CW00829615

SUCCESSFUL
ARTICLE WRITING

THE WRITERS NEWS LIBRARY OF WRITING

No 1 WRITING
Make the Most of Your Time
Kenneth Atchity

No 2 START WRITING TODAY!
Creative Writing for Beginners
André Jute

No 3 PRACTICAL NOVEL WRITING
Dilys Gater

No 4 KEEP ON WRITING!
From Creative Writer to Professional Writer
André Jute

No 5 SHORT STORY WRITING
Dilys Gater

No 6 SUCCESSFUL ARTICLE WRITING
Gillian Thornton

SUCCESSFUL ARTICLE WRITING

Gillian Thornton

DStJT
WN

British Library Cataloguing in Publication Data
Thornton, Gillian
  Successful Article Writing. – ("Writers
  News"Library of Writing; Vol. 6)
  I. Title II. Series
  808

  ISBN 0 946537 86 0 (Hardback)
       0 946537 87 9 (Paperback)

Printed in Great Britain by BPCC Wheatons Ltd, Exeter
for David St John Thomas Publisher,
PO Box 4, Nairn, Scotland IV12 4HU

CONTENTS

Introduction   **7**

1 **Why Magazine Articles?**   **9**
Writing as a hobby · New opportunities · Fact versus
fiction · Essential qualifications · A matter of attitude

2 **Ideas And Where To Find Them**   **20**
Spotting ideas · Keeping an ideas book · Personal
experience · Other sources of ideas · Which one first? ·
Finding an angle

3 **Market Study**   **40**
Who needs it? · Finding new markets · Changes for
the freelance · Starting points · Analysing a
publication · Market information on tap · Aim of the
freelance

4 **Research**   **58**
The familiar and the unfamiliar · Building up your
own library · Using your local library · National
organisations and commercial companies · Cultivating
contacts · Picture research · Information at a price ·
Research through friends

5 **Pen To Paper**   **79**
Man and machine · Working from home · Your
purpose as a writer · Making a synopsis · Beginnings
and endings · Writer's block

6 **A Matter Of Style**   **100**
What is style anyway? · Length · Objectivity ·
Sidebars · Titles · Revision · The moment of truth

CONTENTS

7   **Into The Marketplace**   **118**
    Approaching an editor · Marketing techniques ·
    Rejection can be positive · Acceptance and afterwards ·
    A professional operation

8   **Writing From Experience**   **140**
    Markets and methods · Emotional articles · Humour ·
    How-to · Animals · Travel

9   **Interviewing**   **165**
    Personalities sell · Finding a subject · Finding a
    market · Locating your subject · Making contact ·
    The myths of celebrity interviewing · Doing your
    homework · The night before · On the day ·
    Telephone interviews · Writing it up · Postscript

    Appendix   **188**
    Books referred to in the text

    Index   **189**

INTRODUCTION

I have never forgotten my first sale – an article on bilingual secretaries for a careers magazine nor the kindly editor who politely suggested changes to the manuscript. Little did he know he was launching me on a career which was to bring more job satisfaction than the career I had actually written about.

'I don't know how easy it would be for you to change the article, or indeed if you would be happy to do so,' he wrote, 'but if you could alter certain points, I should be only too pleased to publish it.'

Happy to do so? I would have written it in Chinese if he had asked me. Anything to see my work in print. I made the changes, sent it back within a week, and held my breath till the sae arrived. The article was fine now. Would £8 be acceptable? Oh, yes please! I had done it. I was a writer! I was also hooked.

That was nearly twenty years ago and although I have sold literally hundreds of articles since, I never lose that sense of achievement when I read a feature with my name on it. I have met scores of interesting people, been to hundreds of fascinating places, and – a bonus, in my view – actually been paid for the privilege.

When I first joined a local evening class in creative writing, I had no idea that ordinary mortals such as myself could write for print. But all over the country, there are people like me – and you – doing just that. And being paid for it. With the help of this book, I hope you will soon be one of them, whether you are looking for a second career or simply a way to boost your income.

If you have already sold some of your work, the chapters that follow should help you develop your craft and expand into new markets. The magazine industry – like many others

– has become increasingly competitive in recent years. This book will show you how to stay ahead and establish yourself with editors who pay reliably and well.

Many people have helped and encouraged me along the way, including a number of editors who have known what I could do, even when I did not quite know myself. But four people deserve special thanks – Frank Ferneyhough, who gave me my first lessons in writing for pleasure and profit; my parents, for their steady flow of good ideas; and my husband John, without whose support I would have given up long ago.

ACKNOWLEDGEMENTS

My grateful thanks to Marion Huckle, Librarian at St Albans Central Library, for guiding me through the county library system and providing me with a kit of useful tools for this – and other – projects.

1
WHY MAGAZINE ARTICLES?

WRITING AS A HOBBY

The world is full of aspiring writers. Millions of people write for the sheer joy of expressing themselves on paper, yet a huge number of them remain secret scribblers. They write purely for their own pleasure, never attempting to get their work into print.

Some are simply embarrassed to admit that they like writing, afraid that people will look on it as a rather 'odd' way to spend one's time. So they satisfy their compulsion by filling exercise books with thoughts and observations, only to leave them gathering dust in the back of some forgotten drawer.

Others simply do not realise that there is a market for their work. They think that magazines are all written by staff writers or by experts, and fail to notice the tempting small print at the bottom of the contents page: 'Unsolicited manuscripts should be accompanied by a stamped addressed envelope.'

Unsolicited manuscripts. That means manuscripts which are sent in unasked for. Manuscripts written by people not employed by the publication. Manuscripts written by people like you.

Huge volumes of freelance material are consumed every year by publications large and small. No matter how large the selection in your local newsagent, the magazines arranged neatly on the shelves are just a fraction of the total number produced in Britain today.

There are literally hundreds of other publications that the average consumer never sees – charity magazines and trade journals, small press publications and club magazines.

And if you still doubt whether you could ever be part of that huge, hungry market, then remember that if you have enjoyed writing something, there is a good chance someone else may enjoy reading it. So if you are making the effort to write at all, why not aim for print? Nobody would pretend that it is easy, but it may not be quite as difficult as you think.

Writing has to be the perfect hobby. For a start, you can spend as much or as little time on it as you wish. Practise, of course, makes perfect, and the more you do, the better you will get, but if domestic or work commitments mean you have to down tools for a while, you are unlikely to do long term damage to your literary aspirations.

It is also one of the few hobbies which costs little and can actually earn you money. If you have the time and the talent, the drive and determination, there is no reason why you cannot boost your income by selling your written work or even establish a second career.

After a while, writing becomes a way of life. Even when you are not physically creating something on paper, you can be planning your next piece in your head, dreaming up ideas, or researching market opportunities. Soon you will find that you are doing something creative almost every day.

So you do not need to be tied to the typewriter to be working. As a writer, you can literally go to work at any moment. Often unexpectedly too. If a brilliant idea strikes in the middle of the ironing or while travelling on a train, you can jot it down there and then for future reference.

When you do want to write something up, you can pick a time that fits best with family or work commitments. The busy executive can relax over his typewriter in the evening. A young mum may prefer to write while the children are at school. A person who is unemployed or retired can choose a time when he or she feels most creative.

It may suit you to plan a time when you can work in peace, but you can just as easily seize opportunities as they present themselves. Writing is not like squash or golf, where you must book a slot to enjoy your hobby. You are the boss. There are no demanding employers to see what time you clock in and out and there is no need to feel guilty if you cannot work because of family illness or other commitments.

Self-discipline is obviously important, but you do not have to commit yourself to regular hours. If you cannot afford too much time this week, you can probably catch up next, though chances are you will get so hooked that you will want to make time.

Most hobbies cost money, but it does not cost very much to start work as a writer. Capital outlay is minimal because you are working at home and you do not need much in the way of equipment. You may already own a typewriter, but all you really need in the early days is a large pad and a pencil.

It does not matter if you cannot type – many a Fleet Street journalist has got by perfectly well with two fingers. When you reach the stage of submitting a manuscript to an editor, you will need to get it typed, but most people know some-body who would be willing to help out. If not, you can always take advantage of one of the many low cost typing services which are advertised in the local papers.

If you intend churning out large volumes of copy, you may like to upgrade to a word-processor. They do away with hours of endless retyping so you can edit and re-edit to your heart's content, before printing a perfect manuscript at the touch of a button. But all that comes later. A large blank pad and a good supply of pencils are all you need to launch into your writing career.

Another great advantage of writing as a hobby is that you can combine it with your existing interests and lifestyle. Once you develop an eye for an idea, you will find that material is all around you, just asking to be written up. So if you are bursting to share the ups and downs of domestic life, show people how to master a new skill, or bring your daily work to a wider audience, writing could be for you.

It does all take time of course. Behind every established writer is a path paved with rejection slips, but if you are prepared to persevere and keep practising, the path could be shorter than you think. There is always room for talented new writers and if you have the talent to write and the will to learn, there is no reason why – sooner or later – you should not find your name appearing in the nationals.

Through writing, you will become interested in topics you never knew existed; discover opinions you never knew you had; tap emotions you have never yet experienced. Everyone has hidden talents. Writing articles can bring yours into the open.

New Opportunities

I had just started work as a bilingual secretary when a chance glance at the local paper revived my interest in using my own language. After two years at college studying languages, I was ready to revert to my favourite subject – English – and an evening class in Writing for Pleasure and Profit seemed just the thing.

Not that I considered the Profit angle. After years of writing school essays and critical analyses, I just wanted to enjoy the Pleasure part of the course. But I very nearly gave the Pleasure up on the first evening.

The other students ranged from a young mother to a deputy headmaster, a computer programmer to a retired businessman. What place did I have amongst this articulate crew?

Our tutor advised us to start by writing about what we knew, which presented me with a dilemma. I had taken my first tentative steps into the world of work only weeks earlier. What on earth could I possibly impart of widespread interest?

The only possible option was a careers piece on bilingual secretaries, which I wrote for my first homework. So having made the effort, I went along the second week to hand it in, and the third week to get it back. My tutor liked the feature and helped me shape it, before suggesting I send the manuscript to a glossy careers magazine. The rest you know.

I wrote a second piece, humour this time, about life as a temporary secretary in London. It sold and by the end of the tax year I had amassed a staggering £25 – plus a large pile of rejection slips. But there was no going back.

For several years, writing was just a hobby whilst I carried on my job as personal assistant to a director of a multinational company. But slowly, slowly, the writing began to take over. I began writing for the company newspaper, gained acceptances with a broader range of publications, and finally decided that this was the life for me.

Eventually I took the plunge and went freelance. Now I write anything anybody will buy – general features and celebrity interviews, domestic humour and commercial editorial. I have established myself in a number of regular markets and am in the happy position of having editors ask me for material. I even ended up teaching the writing class which launched me into my new career.

But it is a constant challenge. Editors move on, magazines change and next week I could be needing new markets, so I never get complacent – I am too busy looking for new opportunities. Last year, for instance, I discovered an opening with a DIY magazine. This year, I created a slot for myself in an outdoor leisure title. Next year... who knows? I never have the chance to get bored.

FACT VERSUS FICTION

So why write articles? Why not write short stories or the novel we are all supposed to have inside?

One very good reason is that writing articles is far less time consuming than writing a novel. You can write up to 90 1,000 word articles in the time it takes you to write a 90,000 word novel, allowing extra time, of course, for research or interviews.

That gives you 90 chances of acceptance against one rather remote possibility. The vast majority of first novels end up in the bottom drawer. Every so often, a new writer will be hailed as a sparkling discovery, but for every one who makes it, thousands more are disappointed.

Selling a second novel is even harder nowadays. If the author's first title was not a financial success for the publisher, he is wary of taking the same risk a second time. Could you stand the heartbreak of spending months creating something, only to have it rejected?

13

Write short pieces and you can not only write more of them, you will also learn as you go along. If one piece is rejected several times, you may be able to see why and rewrite it for a different market. The editor may even tell you why your manuscript is not suitable, thereby helping you to avoid the same mistakes next time.

Perhaps you simply sent your piece to the wrong publication. Even successful writers have to keep their market knowledge bang up to date. Magazines often make subtle changes to their content in a bid to maintain their circulation and a potential contributor needs to be aware of those changes.

As an article writer, you can afford to be optimistic. Have several ideas going at the same time – a couple in the planning stage, one in the typewriter, and two or three more out with editors. Then if one comes back with a rejection slip, you still stand a chance with another. Where there is work in progress, there is always hope.

But why not short stories? You can work on several of those at once and they will not take months to complete like a novel.

Just pick up any general interest or woman's magazine and you will immediately find the answer. Count the number of short stories in relation to the number of articles, and you will soon see that the market for articles is far greater than the market for fiction.

That means you have a far greater chance of selling. Especially if you are a novice. There are a great many small or controlled circulation magazines where the pay is low, the competition less great, and the chances of success therefore much higher.

Then there is the question of subject matter. Ideas for articles are all around us – in the things we do and the people we meet, the papers we read and the places we go. There is a huge variety of material to be written about and an equally huge variety of publications hungry to publish it.

Ideas may not come easily to start with, but – as you will see in the next chapter – they soon start to come along with practise. Whatever your age and experience, you will find you have something useful to draw on.

If you are still not sure, just stop and think about the doors that article writing can open – the places you can go and the people you will meet. A good writer is always welcome and there will always be a market for original, entertaining material. The opportunities are yours for the asking.

ESSENTIAL QUALIFICATIONS

So can anybody be a writer? The simple answer is yes. You do not need academic qualifications, not even in written English. If you can speak the language comfortably, then you can write it – perhaps not for *The Times* or the *New Statesman*, but certainly for a less erudite publication (and most of them are less erudite).

A popular chatty style is needed for the majority of national magazines. Sparkle is more important than perfect syntax. Long sentences and unusual words can actually be a disadvantage. No one wants to pick up the dictionary along with their magazine or wrestle with long, unwieldy sentences.

Think of a 'how to' type of article, for instance. Anything from how to tempt a faddy eater, to how to grow better vegetables. The reader wants clear, concise instructions which are easy to follow and which will tempt the reader to try the technique for himself. Remember that and you will always reach your reader.

And how about domestic humour? The reader wants to feel that she is having a conversation with a friend, so the style needs to be chatty. She also wants to be able to relate to the writer and her experiences, and draw parallels with her own family.

One mum's view of her child's first term at 'Big School' will strike a chord with millions of other mothers. If it is amusingly written – or offers some practical advice to other parents – it may find a home with a variety of parentcraft or women's interest magazines.

But although you do not need academic qualifications to be a writer, it does help to ask yourself a few basic questions, before you rush out for a secondhand typewriter. Like most things that are worth doing, a certain amount of hard work and application are vital if you are going to make a success of writing.

– Do you enjoy writing long, chatty letters detailing all the family happenings? If you have lots to say but prefer to use the telephone, writing may not be for you.

– Are you full of ideas? Do you look at things with a writer's eye and find sentences come unasked into your head? It is not enough just being able to write, you must have something to write about.

– Do you have any specialised knowledge? Your job, perhaps, your hobby, or your family? If the answer is yes, you have a ready source of material from which to start.

– Do you enjoy finding out, either by researching material from books or asking people for information? Depending on what sort of pieces you want to write, you may need to visit libraries or talk to individuals for information.

– Are you thorough with a logical mind? Written work needs to be logically laid out and thoroughly revised, if it is to find a market.

– Do you love words? Writers need to make words work for them and that means not always choosing the first one that springs to mind.

– Are you determined? There will be rejections along the way – perhaps many of them – before that first acceptance. Have you got what it takes to carry on?

– Are you willing to make time? Articles do not write themselves. Will you find the time, however fragmented and however long it takes?

– Do you like people? Article writers meet a lot of them. Or are you happier working on your own?

16

If your answer to most of these questions is yes, then you have plenty of promising qualities. All you need now is to learn the basic techniques.

People often ask if it is possible to teach someone to be a writer. Obviously some people have more natural flair than others, but there is no reason why anyone cannot learn the principles of writing for publication. I have taught college students and senior citizens, young mums and middle managers to improve their writing technique and many of them have gone on to see their work in print.

A MATTER OF ATTITUDE

Your attitude to writing is a vital factor in your chance of success. Some people are embarrassed to say they write, especially if they are unpublished. But everyone has to start somewhere and if you do not take yourself seriously, you cannot expect anyone else to.

Other people have a romantic idea of what writing is all about. It is not enough just to jot a few ideas down and tell everyone you are a writer. You are not a writer till you have finished a manuscript. So you must have a goal in mind, however easy it may be to reach.

Ask yourself what motivates you as a writer. Is it love, money or a bit of both? Most writers start scribbling out of sheer enjoyment. After all, if you did not enjoy it, creating a piece of written work would be self-inflicted torture.

But if editors like your work, the question of money is going to come into it sooner or later. Never be ashamed to say you write for money. You can still enjoy your writing. It just means that you are now accepting realistic reward for your efforts. And why not? You do not have to starve in a garrett to be a 'real' writer.

Real writers must learn not to get depressed by the bad days. There will be days when the words just will not come, days when you have not got time to write, and days when your cherished manuscript comes thudding back on to the doormat. Every writer has them – even experienced, successful writers. The important thing is not to let them get you down.

Many people find that an action plan written and hung over the typewriter gives them the boost to keep going. Simply decide on a goal of so many words per week or so many hours at the keyboard. Then cross them off as each milestone is achieved.

Once you have some marketable ideas to develop, list them on your chart so you can move triumphantly on to the next title, once the current production is safely in the post. Keep adding ideas to the chart, so you always have plenty of projects to work on.

But do set yourself realistic targets and do not punish yourself by trying to attain the impossible. Writing is supposed to be fun. It is all very well to aim for quantity, so long as the writing is good, but quality is what sells in the marketplace. Aim at 1,000 words a week and get there, rather than 5,000 words and fail.

Incentives are important too, especially in the early days when the prospect of acceptance and a cheque seems a long way off. A sense of achievement is all very well until the manuscript you pinned your hopes on comes back with a rejection slip. So give yourself small rewards for targets reached. That way you have something to look forward to if the manuscript does not sell.

Take every opportunity to learn your craft and get to know the industry in which you work. If you are going to sell your articles, you need to know what editors want and how to give it to them. So study *Writers News* magazine every month for tips, techniques and a wealth of information about new and existing markets.

Make an effort to meet other writers too. Ask at your local library or consult the pages of *Writers News* for details of your nearest writers circle. There you will meet other people from all walks of life with the same aspirations as your own.

Writers are a friendly bunch who are only too happy to share their ups and downs with other like-minded souls. Complete beginners will pick up lots of valuable tips from experienced members, whilst established writers can keep abreast of market changes by swapping experiences.

If there is no group in your area, start one. An advertisement in *Writers News*, your local library or community centre could be enough to bring in a nucleus of members. Many well established writers circles which began by meeting in each other's homes are now big enough to need rented accommodation.

They arrange speakers, organise workshops, and run competitions. Above all, they provide moral support and advice for people who have chosen to follow what can be a rather solitary occupation. It is all too easy to get despondent if your articles are being rejected and you do not know why.

So if you are short of ideas, low on confidence, or dying to share your latest literary success, go along to a writers circle – you are sure to come home with your head buzzing and renewed energy to start work again tomorrow.

2
IDEAS AND WHERE TO FIND THEM

SPOTTING IDEAS

Ideas are the first major stumbling block for any writer. All the writing talent in the world will not help you, if you cannot think of anything to write about. Very few novices are lucky enough to find ideas coming thick and fast. One or two may spring to mind, but after that, it is nothing short of hard graft... until you get the knack.

Finish your very first piece and you may be surprised at the mixed feelings that follow. You will almost certainly be elated at having completed your first piece of potentially saleable work, but you may also be horrified at the prospect of having nothing else to write about. You have worked through your one idea, so which way now?

Do not panic. Ideas are all around us and the determined writer can soon learn to cultivate a nose for ideas. In no time at all, you will find you have almost more ideas than you can realistically cope with. Then you are in the fortunate position of being able to choose the ones which appeal to you most or the ones which seem most likely to sell.

There are four important words to remember about becoming an ideas sleuth: LOOK – LISTEN – ENQUIRE – EXPLORE.

LOOK – Keep your eyes open wherever you go. Marketable ideas crop up in the most unexpected places. You do not always have to seek out the rare and unusual. Many stories get ignored simply because they seem too obvious. Do not automatically assume that a subject has been covered. Even if it has, you may find a different angle.

LISTEN – Take notice of conversations around you. Listen

to strangers talking on buses and in waiting rooms. Tune in to television and radio. Wherever there are people talking, make sure you are unobtrusively listening to what they say.

ENQUIRE – Ask questions. About places you visit, people you meet, subjects that interest you. You will be amazed how quickly one topic can lead into another, one idea suddenly expand to make several.

EXPLORE – Be adventurous. Take every opportunity that comes your way to increase your range of experiences. You may not see a market for a subject now, but few experiences are ever wasted. And if nothing exciting comes your way, explore topics from your own armchair – look at opposites, alternatives, firsts and lasts, youngest and oldest. The possibilities are endless.

If you are still stuck, try brainstorming. Pick up the nearest paper or magazine and choose a subject at random. Let us say there is an article about a new motorway. How many related ideas can you think of?

The first British motorway – from drawing board to the present day.
How motorways have changed the face of travel.
Motorways of the future.
Tips for travelling with children.
Wildlife along the motorways.
How to improve your motorway driving.
Life without motorways.
Motorway catering.

These are just a few ideas. Some of them could be written from different angles for different markets. Some could even be humorous. Here is another subject – portrait painters:

Artists of our time.
Royal portraits through the ages.
Taking up painting.
Opportunities for artists' models.
Art appreciation for adults.
A visit to an art gallery.

Teaching children about art.
Working from home – the pleasures and pitfalls.

Of course some of these ideas would be more difficult to write up than others, just as some might prove more difficult to sell, but brainstorming is an excellent way of training yourself to spot potentially marketable ideas.

KEEPING AN IDEAS BOOK

Never dismiss an idea, however unlikely it may seem at the time. You never know when the brainwave you had on the bus or the ideas you brainstormed in the bath one evening will come in handy.

Once you start venturing into the marketplace, you will want to approach editors with ideas for articles, and the more ideas you can offer, the more chance you will have of a sale. Used in conjunction with your cuttings book – find out how in Chapter 3 – you will have starting points for a whole bank of saleable material.

So set up an ideas book and get into the habit of using it right from the start. An indexed notebook is ideal, inexpensive, and readily available from high street stationers. File ideas by subject, cross referencing where appropriate, so you do not miss any opportunity to expand on a given subject.

Underneath each idea, make notes of any potential contacts who could provide more information. You should also refer to any background material you may have in your own files – newspaper cuttings, for example, or notes taken from the radio or television.

Chapter 4 takes a closer look at research sources, but if you get in the habit of linking ideas and information from the outset, you will be establishing the basis for efficient article production.

Refer to your ideas book regularly. An idea you did not rate very highly when you wrote it down may suddenly have become marketable in the light of recent events or because it ties in with a particular market at which you are now aiming.

Your ideas book will also provide you with hours of valuable writing practise. Whenever you want to write but have nothing specific to write about, thumb through the pages until you find something that appeals. Not only will you be improving your writing techniques, you may also find a subject that turns out to be far more fascinating than you first thought.

If you are still not sure you can find enough subjects for your articles, stop and consider some of the different ways of generating ideas.

PERSONAL EXPERIENCE

Personal experience pieces are an excellent way to start. Everyone has something interesting to tell as a direct result of their own lives – some aspect of their job, for example, a holiday experience or hobby technique, a personal crisis overcome, or a humorous tale of family life.

If you can write from experience, you can write with authority and if you can write with authority, an editor will look more favourably on your manuscript. And – important to both novice and experienced writer alike – if you are writing about something you enjoy and feel confident about, you will almost certainly find you write better.

Chapter 8 looks at various techniques for writing some of the most popular types of personal experience article, but first you need to sit down and brainstorm some potentially saleable ideas. Let us look at the lives of two aspiring writers, Jenny and Tom, to see what personal experiences they could draw on.

> Jenny is married with two young children. Her husband runs a publicity business from home and Jenny helps him with secretarial work. She enjoys tennis, swimming, and going out and about with the children. Once her daughter starts school, Jenny hopes to train for a new career, perhaps something involving children. Her son suffers from asthma and was taken into hospital last year during a bad attack. The family enjoy caravanning holidays and recently bought their own caravan.

Jenny has a variety of experiences she could write about. See how many you can think of before you read the list below.

– Age gaps. What sort of sibling spacing works best? (Her children are four years apart, but her friends will have different gaps. What are the pros and cons of each gap?)

– Preparing your child for school. (Her son is six and has just completed his first year in full-time education. What can parents do to help?)

– When husband works from home. (Pros and cons. This could be factual, humorous or, better still, yield two articles for different markets.)

– Earning money while the children are young. (Jenny works for her husband, but what other ways are there of earning money with small children underfoot?)

– Sports for tiny tots. (Jenny plays tennis and swims – perhaps her children do too. How and where to teach them. What it will cost. Equipment needed. Could make two separate articles – one tennis, one swimming – or one more general one about physical activities for tinies.)

– Going back to work. (Jenny wants to retrain. How does she find out what is available to her? Who can help her choose the right course and career? Regaining confidence after staying at home with children. Lots of potential here from a number of different angles.)

– Careers with children. (She is going to be finding out what is available, so why not share the information?)

– Living with asthma. (Passing on her experience of coping with her son.)

– Children in hospital. (What to expect. How to prepare them.)

– Caravanning with children. (Tips for happy holidays in close proximity).

– Choosing a caravan. (How to choose the best one for your needs. The features you really need and the ones you can live without.)

– Location reports. Where to go with your caravan. Perhaps a series along a chosen theme.

Well, there are twelve ideas to start with. You can probably think of more. Now what about Tom?

> Tom retired last year from the engineering company where he worked for 30years. He and his wife moved to the seaside to be near their son and his family, after first taking an extended motoring holiday on the continent. Tom already enjoys making and flying model aeroplanes, but has just enrolled for painting classes at the local college. He is also keen on keeping fit and wants to take up some new sports.

Much older than Jenny, with a totally different lifestyle, Tom still has a wide range of topics which he could write about with authority. For example:

– Getting ready for retirement. (Most big companies offer their employees advice in how to make the most out of retirement. If Tom was not offered such advice, he may well have attended a course run by his local further education college. Failing that, he is bound to have tips of his own, so why not pass them on?)

– The changing face of engineering. (The profession has altered dramatically in 30 years. Today's young engineers could be interested to hear Tom's experiences of the 'old days'. Or perhaps a piece for his company's in-house newspaper.)

– Moving to a new area. (Tom and his wife have left the

friends they made during 30 years in one area. How have they adapted? Was it a good idea? Have they been able to make new friends? What advice can they offer?)

– How to be a good grandad. (Tom has grandchildren, so write about them. A light-hearted, but informative piece on how to be a good grandparent, or perhaps a humorous piece on a day out with the grandchildren.)

– Motoring on the continent. (Perhaps aimed at Senior Citizens. Travel tips, itineraries and recommendations, liberally sprinkled with anecdotes.)

– Model aeroplanes. (There are many model magazines on the market. Tom could pick specific aspects of his hobby and write 'how to' articles for specialist publications.)

– Taking up a retirement hobby. (Tom fancies painting. Where can he go to learn? What else could be take up? What would it cost?)

– Keeping fit in retirement. (Importance of keeping fit. Diet. Exercise. Sporting activities.)

Now we have eight potentially saleable ideas for Tom too. Only hope Jenny and Tom like writing! Neither of them comes from any particular social background. They do not have any special privileges, nor have they made a name for themselves in any particular field. They are ordinary people, who nevertheless have valuable experience to pass on.

So sit down and ask yourself a few basic questions about:

Your family.
Your training and career.
Unpaid work
Hobbies
Pets
Holidays

Domestic crises such as illness, death, crime victim, accidents, and so on.

Then look for article ideas in each answer. You should get at least one idea from each. Still dubious? Let me prove it. These are just a few examples of the sort of personal experience pieces I have sold:

Family

I am married with two young children. Almost every stage of their development has yielded at least one article for a national magazine, often more.

I have sold a wide variety of childcare and behaviour features, as well as domestic humour, to both mother and baby magazines and general interest women's magazines. Coping with toddler tantrums, for instance. What is the best age to have children? How to get your figure back after a baby.

With no brothers or sisters of my own, I have written about the pros and cons of only children, even tracking down a number of celebrities for their views on the subject. I have also written up my childhood memories. Yes, growing up in the 50s and 60s is fascinatingly old-fashioned nowadays!

Training and Career

I started life as a bilingual secretary, began writing as a hobby, worked in public relations for a hotel group, and joined the staff of a big company newspaper, before becoming a self-employed journalist.

I have written several pieces on working from home – how I do it, how others do it, what options are available, and so on – as well as features on changing careers, office politics, and other aspects of working life. I have taught writing at evening class and written about that too. Markets? Almost everywhere – careers magazines, women's titles, and even trade magazines.

Unpaid work

Do you do any voluntary work? Have you organised a fete or a charity function? Do you serve on a club committee or parent/teacher association? I have sold articles on teaching adults, running a writers circle and amateur fund-raising.

Hobbies

How do you fill your leisure time? I ride, swim, and go out with my children. One of my favourite rides is along the five miles of off-road tracks opened up by a local farmer – a topical and original article for one of the specialist horse magazines.

I have written about a weekend course in heavy horse driving and a trailriding holiday on the Welsh borders – both given to me free as press trips. I have investigated swimming courses for adults and compiled several themed articles on outings with children.

Pets

A tricky one, this, as you will appreciate in Chapter 8. Our pets are always special to us, but will they be to other people? You will need to be very objective in deciding whether you really have something original to pass on. But there is a market for petcare and animal experience pieces, and an even broader market for features on animal charities and personalities – whether two-legged or four.

I have sold features on Battersea Dogs Home, The National Canine Defence League, and other well known organisations, as well as on animal artists, famous conservationists and unusual rescue centres.

Holidays

How lovely to make your holidays pay for themselves. Unfortunately, travel writing is rarely as easy as it looks – see Chapter 8 for some tips – but if you have an eye for the unusual and are prepared to do some homework before you go, you may unearth some good article ideas at your holiday destination.

One family holiday yielded a travel article, two celebrity interviews and a general feature which sold to two national women's titles and an in-flight magazine, thus paying for the entire holiday. In fact the local tourist board subsequently invited me back on an all-expenses-paid press trip.

Domestic Crises

We all have them, but can we turn a negative experience into a positive and saleable one? My husband and son suffer from inherited high cholesterol, which involves following a low-fat diet. I accumulated so much expert information on the condition, that I wrote – and sold – three features written in layman's terms to non-competitive magazines.

And when my car was written off in an accident – nearly taking me with it – I wrote an emotional piece for a woman's magazine about the way it had affected my outlook on life. Therapeutic and profitable.

OTHER SOURCES OF IDEAS

Newspapers

There is no copyright on ideas, only on the way in which they are written up. So you are quite free to lift ideas from other publications so long as you write them in your own words. In fact local and national newspapers are an excellent source of material for article writers.

Look for the story behind those eye-catching photographs at which the national dailies excel. In one, for example, a row of children had been arranged in ascending order of height from a baby in a bouncing chair to a twelve-year-old in school uniform.

The caption underneath revealed they were all pupils at a new school set up to cater for working parents, the first of its kind to take youngsters from tots to teens. An ideal subject for a general woman's magazine or childcare publication.

Local papers can be even more fruitful. Unusual small businesses, artists and craftsmen, local celebrities, places to visit – the opportunities are many and varied. There are often enough details given in the write-up for you to track the subject down through the local phone book. If not, ring the news desk of the relevant paper and ask for information.

Magazines

Like newspapers, magazines are an excellent source of article ideas. A feature in a specialist title could be slanted towards a more general interest magazine; a news snippet expanded into a major feature; or a subject simply recycled for another market.

Support Groups

Most local papers publish a regular list of support groups in the area. Everything from organisations for harrassed parents to those dealing with specific illnesses or conditions. Many of these have wider appeal and the organisers are always eager for more exposure, especially if you are aiming at the national press.

Similarly, if you hear about a national organisation on television that interests you, contact their headquarters for the name of your nearest branch. You might then be able to angle a national network to a local market.

Perhaps there are schools for children with special needs in your area or you know someone whose child suffers from a particular condition. Most individuals and organisations in these circumstances are only too happy to help make people aware of the problem and thus, perhaps, raise extra funds or attract more volunteer help.

Libraries

Libraries also carry lists of local support groups, societies, clubs, and voluntary organisations. Study their noticeboard regularly and watch for free leaflets about what is going on in your area.

They can also help with local history. Most major libraries carry back issues of local papers and magazines, as well as books about the area. Some of the older volumes may well reveal unexpected information about some aspect of local life in days gone by – always of interest to county magazines and sometimes even national titles. But do double-check your information wherever possible – facts may vary from one source to another, especially when gleaned from old newspapers.

Do not forget the rewards of browsing either. Stroll your fingers along the spines in an unfamiliar section of the library. Inspiration may strike quicker than you think. If you do not already know the full range of library services on offer, Chapter 4 will help you make the most of your local facility.

Television And Radio

Anyone who broadcasts on television or radio is given national exposure, which gives you, the writer, a very good chance of selling a piece about them.

Celebrities are actually not that difficult to get hold of – more of that in Chapter 9 – and very few are averse to a little extra publicity. So watch out for personable presenters, attractive actresses and dishy disc-jockeys. If you think they are good, chances are millions of other viewers or listeners do too.

Watch out for news items, especially on the magazine and discussion programmes. Some of the daytime television shows are an excellent source of topical ideas. Listen to a studio discussion and use it as a basis for an article. Or follow up an interesting place or event which merits just a brief mention on the national airwaves. If you want to know more, so too will other people.

Conversations

All people are interesting to some degree or other, so use what they have to offer. When you meet someone at a party, conduct a little informal interview – without them realising it, of course. Find out what they do for a living, what their hobbies are, where they go on holiday. People like talking about themselves. Listen to what they say and you could find they provide you with a starting point for your next article, perhaps even with the whole article.

Listen to conversations going on around you. Two old ladies chatting about the price of meat on the bus might start you off on an investigation into the way our shopping habits have changed over the years, or a discussion on value for money.

And do not forget those chance remarks that crop up on the domestic front. 'What is the most romantic thing I have ever done?' a friend's husband asked one night as they watched a romantic comedy on television. The hilarious conversation that followed turned into an article about finding the perfect anniversary present.

Women's Interest

It is possible to find a woman's angle in almost anything. Social issues, politics, hobbies, activities. The list is endless. How are working mothers affected, for example, by lack of childcare provision? What opportunities are there for women in male-dominated careers? Pose the questions and then set out to find the answers. And you do not have to be a woman to write it.

Individual incidents often provide the basis for a feature, without necessarily being the subject of the piece. Consider the questions raised by your partner's career, for example. Do you resent his success? (Or hers? That would be a good feature!) How are couples affected by each other's jobs?

Suppose that you go away for a weekend on your own. Chaos reigns when you get home. Or perhaps everything is in perfect order. So could your partner manage without you? All sorts of article opportunities there...

Similarly, you have crashed the car/lost your job/trodden on the hamster. How do you break the news? That feature could be humorous, contemplative, even tragic. Look for a common feeling in things that happen to you and you may have the basis for a feature that will appeal to a wide audience.

Letters Pages

Letters pages provide plenty of ideas which can be turned into full-length articles. Letters to general interest magazines cover everything from overheard conversation to social comment, opinions about items in the magazine to useful tips. Specialist titles are more subject-related.

Other People's Jobs

You can often make money out of somebody else's job or hobby. Unusual occupations are always marketable. A couple who breed thousands of edible snails in the front room. The elderly gentleman who runs a shirt-ironing service. Or the lady sewage specialist who has, on occasions, fallen right in up to her neck.

Small businesses can also make good copy. How and why they were set up. The struggle for finance. The battle against the giants. Personal service versus big chain anonymity. This type of story appeals to a variety of large markets, from general interest magazines through to business publications and specialist titles covering a particular product or activity.

Anniversaries And Topical Events

Every year has its anniversaries. Some make national headlines, others are hardly mentioned. Unless you have a particularly original angle on a big story, it is probably best to aim for something which is not likely to attract so much media attention. Then create that attention yourself.

Topicality is vital here and lead times need to be taken into account – see Chapter 7 for help in timing your submissions. As for subjects, you will find plenty of inspiration in the listings carried each year by the *Writers' & Artists' Yearbook*,

Whitaker's Almanac, or a good dictionary of dates. More about sources of information in Chapter 4.

Cuttings

Once you get the ideas habit, you will soon find you cannot read a magazine or newspaper without spotting potential for other articles. Try looking at a topic from a different angle, expanding a small item into a feature, or doing a follow-up piece. But again, do remember the importance of topicality. Old news is no news and that, for the writer, means no sale.

Build up your own cuttings library with the help of Chapter 3. As well as ensuring that you have information readily available on your particular areas of interest, it will prove a valuable source of article ideas.

Never miss an opportunity to study the market and add to your information store. Few writers can afford to subscribe to more than a few papers or periodicals, but there are plenty of other ways to ensure you see a wide variety of publications.

Try the reading room of your local library and always arrive early at the doctor, dentist or hairdresser to make the most of the reading matter on offer. Arrange a regular magazine swap with friends, family and other writers, and watch for bundles of magazines at car boot sales and jumble sales.

Holidays And Outings

Holidays and excursions can provide the freelance writer with a wealth of article opportunities from travel pieces to general features and personality pieces.

Ask the tourist board for information leaflets before you travel and borrow some regional guides from your local library. Hunt through your own cuttings library, in case you have a local story or personality piece on file.

And do not forget to track down the name of any county magazine or regional publication which may provide a suitable market later. If you phone the editor and explain that you are a journalist, they may even be prepared to send you a back copy free of charge for research.

Outings and places to visit can also provide the freelance with feature material. Compilation features crop up time after time – Ten Top Theme Parks, The Best of British Zoos, Stately Homes for all the Family, and so on.

But try looking for the slightly more unusual story. An interview with someone behind the scenes, an unusual event or little known personality link. The angle you choose can make all the difference between success and rejection.

Free Literature

Everyone complains about junk mail, but free literature can often bring money rolling in for the feature writer. Go to any major exhibition, for example, and you will probably come home with carrier bags full of booklets and brochures. You certainly cannot keep them all, but before you consign them to the bin, sift through very selectively and keep anything which might come in useful later. If in doubt, do not throw out.

Particularly useful are addresses of contacts. So if, for example, you have accumulated a pile of literature on conservatories, you could keep one or two brochures from key manufacturers or suppliers, together with the names, addresses and phone numbers of other firms to contact if required. Result? A potential sale to a home interest magazine.

Advertisements

Magazine advertisements and television commercials can sometimes spark off article ideas. The story behind a particularly appealing advertisement, for instance. Or something about advertising itself – changing styles or perhaps an opinion piece about the tone or content of today's advertisements.

Mailing Lists

One article often leads to another – sometimes unexpectedly.

If you come into contact with someone during the course of researching one article, always make sure they have your details on file for future reference.

Public relations companies, for example, often handle a very broad range of clients and may well be able to offer you other article opportunities. Find out who else they are promoting and ask to be put on their mailing list for press information. They will not want to miss the chance of more publicity.

Similarly, if you are in touch with the press office of a television company or radio station, ask if they are promoting any other programmes in the near future. You might just be the first to scoop an interview.

Publishers' Catalogues

If you like the idea of doing author interviews, phone round the publishers for a free copy of their catalogue. Most publish them twice yearly and they carry brief details of forthcoming titles together with biographical information about the authors.

Many authors are available for interview and publishers' press offices are only too glad to set them up for you. Publicity budgets are limited and feature writers are made very welcome. You will also get an advance copy of the book for review.

Statistics

The papers are full of them. Population. Marriages. Traffic. Accidents. Births. Deaths. Animal cruelty. Do not just see them as numbers. Look at the story behind them.

If there is a dramatic change in the divorce figures, for example, you could interview a local marriage counsellor or perhaps talk to divorced couples. If there is been a big reduction in the number of abandoned pets, visit a rescue centre for their view of the story.

WHICH ONE FIRST?

Lucky is the writer who has to choose which idea to tackle first. There are days when even the most experienced writer has no choice but to knuckle down to a subject he does not particularly like.

But if you do have a choice, should you automatically go for the one you like best? Not always. If you really want to sell, you should always write the most topical story first. There might be other journalists out there with the same idea. Make sure your article is the first on the editor's desk – and the best.

After that, go for a topic you know well or care deeply about. If you are enthusiastic about a subject, you will be keen to write it well and motivated to see it through. From the sales point of view, it is also sensible to tackle any subject which has broad reader appeal – it is far more likely to find favour with an editor if he knows it will interest the majority of his readers rather than just a select few.

FINDING AN ANGLE

Once you have the germ of an idea, you will need to decide on your angle. If you are writing about model railways, for example, you will write differently for a magazine catering for young modellers than you will for a publication aimed at an experienced adult readership.

The angle you choose will therefore depend largely on the market you are writing for, which is why it is important to do your market research thoroughly. So until you have chosen your target publication – with the help of Chapter 3 – you will need to be flexible about your chosen topic. Do not decide on your approach until you know exactly who you are going to be writing for.

Of course you may be writing for more than one market. There is always a variety of ways to approach a given subject and article writers should train themselves to look for multiple angles from each idea. It is amazing how many potentially saleable pieces never get written just because the writer thinks he has used up that idea after one sale.

So focus your thoughts on a specific angle or – even better – several different angles. You may be able to write one subject from a variety of angles or write one angle for a variety of non-competitive publications.

Take this example. A stately home open to the public also incorporates a farm specialising in rare breeds of farm animals. So what potential is there here for the feature writer?

A tour of the farm for a children's magazine.
A behind-the-scenes piece for a woman's magazine.
Rare breeds for an animal magazine.
Stately homes with animal attractions for a parentcraft
    magazine.
A topical profile for the local county magazine.
Farming methods old and new for an agricultural title.

You can probably think of some more, but there are six different angles from one basic idea. And you could probably get enough information to write all of them from just one visit.

It is perfectly acceptable to recycle the same material, so long as you do not use exactly the same words and are aiming at non-competitive markets. Your days as a freelance contributor could be numbered if you offered similar pieces to editors of magazines aimed at the same readership, but with the wealth of titles in print today, you should not be short of good markets.

Take another example, sparked off by a short news item in a national newspaper. Some hibernating hedgehogs were apparently in danger of dying in their sleep, simply because they were too skinny. The staff of an animal rescue centre were therefore nudging them awake and feeding them on dogfood. Short and poignant, but with lots of potential for the feature writer:

An interview with the people running the rescue centre,
    written up for both an animal magazine and a women's
    publication.

A feature on animals that hibernate for a children's publication.

A look at wildlife rescue centres round the country for a
women's or general interest publication.

Caring for wildlife at home, again with several possible
markets.

Focussing your attention on specific angles will open up a
wealth of new market opportunities. Few magazines, for
example, would be interested in a general travel article on
London, but many editors might consider a piece on
Children's London, London's Hidden Museums, or London
for the Disabled.

A strong angle will not only help you to sell your work, it
will also help you to write tight copy with no wasted words or
unnecessary anecdotes. When you know which direction you
are going in – what information to put in and what to leave
out – you will make the whole process of article production
much more efficient.

So ask yourself questions around each topic, keep each one
on file, and then sit down to do your market research.

3
MARKET STUDY

WHO NEEDS IT?

You do. Whether you are writing features or fillers, a series of articles or a single reader's letter, there is one basic rule to remember if you really want to sell your work. Market before manuscript.

No matter how brilliant your idea, how original your style, you stand a far better chance of placing your copy if you choose your target publication before you put pen to paper.

Editors of popular magazines receive scores of unsolicited manuscripts every week, but only a small percentage of those on the 'slush pile' are likely to find their way into print. Most publications are written largely by staff writers or by freelances whose work is already known to the editor.

So the would-be contributor needs to target his work very carefully. His copy needs to stand out from the competition and that means convincing the editor that he wrote the article with just one publication in mind.

One of the most common faults amongst novice writers is inadequate market study. Just because a range of magazines are grouped together under Women's Interest in the newsagent, they assume they all appeal to the same type of reader. But every one has a specific readership. It exists to serve a particular market segment and although it may overlap other titles in subject matter, the treatment will always be different.

Market study is just as important to the experienced journalist. Magazines frequently revamp their style and content to attract new readers in the face of increasing competition. Editors change and with them the type of material they require. Writers need to keep up with these changes if they are to find new markets and retain those with which they are already successful.

Even established journalists need to watch out for ways to expand their market base. The aim of any serious freelance is to sell regularly to markets who pay reliably and well, but markets do fall by the wayside. Magazines close down and the regular contributor who once seemed so secure is suddenly left with a hole in his income and a batch of ideas all going to waste.

An ideal set-up for a serious freelance would be to establish himself as a regular contributor – a 'staff freelance' if you like – to perhaps three or four national magazines, spanning a variety of markets. In addition, he should be constantly on the lookout for one-off sales.

This would provide him with both a varied workload and a healthy income. However, editorial or policy changes may mean that he suddenly loses a regular market which has taken perhaps a dozen or more articles from him every year. Market study then becomes vital to his future as a freelance – not to mention his bank balance.

So your first task as a potential contributor is not to produce a manuscript. It is to decide where that manuscript should go. Your finished article may not, of course, be accepted by your target market for a variety of reasons we will be exploring later on, but if you have studied the market as a whole, you should be able to rewrite and retarget the piece towards another title.

FINDING NEW MARKETS

If you normally shop at a local newsagent with a limited range of publications, it is worth taking a trip to a large shopping centre where you will find a wider range of titles.

Take careful note of the specialist titles, such as sports, hobbies, and professional journals. If you have a particular interest or expertise, look out all the magazines that cover it. You probably will not be able to buy all of them, but you could perhaps purchase one or two of the most appropriate titles.

It is worth remembering that magazines bought for research purchases can be offset against any income you make from writing on your tax return – more of that in Chapter 7 – so keep the receipts and make sure you jot down your expenses in a record book.

But not all magazines appear on the bookstalls. In fact the ones you see displayed in your local high street newsagent, however large, represent only a small proportion of the titles which are published regularly in this country.

If you are just starting out on your writing career, it is unwise to head straight for the big circulation nationals. Unless you are exceptionally talented, you are unlikely to make the grade at the first attempt. Your best bet is to start small and aim for a title with a smaller circulation. The pay will not be great, but neither will the competition. So get one step ahead by searching out titles which other writers may have over-looked.

Even if you are already established as a working journalist, it is well worth tracking down some less well known publications. You may be able to write a spin-off from an article you have researched for a more mainstream publication and earn a little extra money for very little extra effort. You may also find, as a professional, that you can turn your hand to a subject or market area you have never considered – and enjoy it.

Some of the trade publications and other specialist titles pay surprisingly well, especially to a reliable freelance who can produce quality copy to a deadline. And once you have found one new market, you will be surprised how others often seem to land in your lap.

A quick glance through the *Writers' & Artists' Yearbook* or *The Writer's Handbook* will reveal a range of titles which should intrigue any enterprising freelance – *Achievement*, *Ballroom Dancing Times*, and *Community Care* through to *World Outlook* and *The Young Soldier*. A few enquiries amongst friends and colleagues could well reveal others:

In-House Magazines

Many companies, large and small, produce their own in-house publications. Anything from a photocopied news-sheet to a tabloid newspaper or glossy magazine. Some are produced for internal consumption only, whilst others are aimed at customers and business associates.

If you already work for a company with a newspaper of its own, offer your services as a correspondent. Most editors work alone or with a small team, so they are pleased to accept news and views from around the company, especially from somebody who can write.

One valuable tip to remember when writing any news story is to convey your various points in decreasing order of importance. News items are always cut from the bottom up, whereas a feature article may be edited at any point.

Writing for company newspapers can provide valuable practise in the art of producing tight copy. There is no room for wasted words when there are other topical stories to be squeezed onto a busy page. But there can be spin-offs too.

One novice, but talented, young writer working in the health and safety department of a large manufacturing company, began by offering a feature to his own company newspaper. Spurred on by his initial success, he then approached the magazine of a health and safety organisation with his own unique view of pollution. Not only did they accept it, but they asked him to produce a regular series covering the history of pollution control in various British industries. All at very acceptable rates of pay, plus expenses for UK travel.

Ironically, he had begun his writing career by penning short stories, but, finding them difficult to sell, had decided to try articles instead. Now he is completely hooked, both by the variety of his work and the level of his success.

Even if you do not have in-house connections, you may still be able to write for a company publication. Do you have a story to tell about a company's products or services from the consumer point of view? Do you have any interest or expertise which may overlap the area in which a particular company works? An enquiry to the editor may result in an invitation to submit your work.

Trade Magazines

If you can find your way into an in-house publication, you may

43

also be able to move into trade journals. These are magazines covering not a particular company, but a whole industry – *Dairy Farmer*, *Electrical Review* and *Studio Sound*, for instance.

Some are listed in the *Writers' & Artists' Yearbook*, but you should consult one of the media directories outlined in Chapter 4 for a more complete list. Some of the magazines are available on controlled circulation to managers and decision makers or by subscription only, rather than on the bookstalls, but if you phone the editor and explain why you want to study his magazine, he may send you a back copy or two.

Some trade journals require very high standards of journalism and pay accordingly, making them a lucrative market for experienced writers. But others are less worried about the writing, so long as the information is accurate. All you can do is try them and see.

Try looking for a local angle to a national issue. Product-related articles are usually handled in-house or by experts, but if you can find a people angle or a new local venture, you might be in with a good chance.

Freebies

Free magazines and newspapers are a relatively recent phenomenon in the publishing world. Delivered to the door or distributed at selected outlets, they make their money through the number of advertisers they attract, rather than the number of papers they sell.

Most towns have at least one free local paper. Some may have four or five. They do, of course, have their own editorial staff, but if you have an inside angle on a local story, they may be happy to let you have a go. Phone the news desk with your idea and be ready to go. Deadlines are tight on a weekly paper.

Then there are the free magazines distributed by airlines and ferry companies, hotel groups and other commercial organisations. Some of them are almost as well known as the major bookstall titles – and just as difficult to get into. One major airline magazine, for instance, accepts no unsolicited manuscripts and will not even consider ideas. Unless, of course, you happen to be a Very Famous Name indeed.

However, the prospect is not all doom and gloom. There is always the occasional opening for the writer who can offer something a little out of the ordinary which exactly suits the market.

Club Magazines

Many clubs, societies and organisations run their own limited circulation publications – parish magazines, club newsletters, school magazines, and so on. Editors are usually voluntary and unpaid, so should be glad of some ready-made copy.

And if you are a member of an organisation which does not have some sort of communications bulletin, suggest one – with yourself as editor, of course. You will not make any money, but you will make friends and gain some valuable writing experience into the bargain. Do not worry if you have no experience – chances are, nobody else will have either.

If you are a member of a local writers group, you may already have placed work in a club anthology. Some are distributed solely amongst members and their friends, whilst others are sold through local bookshops. Just one word of warning – if an article has been reproduced in this way, it may not be eligible for external competitions which demand unpublished work. If in doubt, keep your masterpiece back and write something else for the club booklet.

CHANGES FOR THE FREELANCE

Despite the recent economic recession, a lot of new magazines have found their way onto the bookstalls. Some of course have gone, but there is certainly no shortage of publications to try.

The *Writers' & Artists' Yearbook* or *The Writer's Handbook* should give you plenty more market ideas, but remember that these volumes, useful though they are, should only ever be used as a basis for further market study. They go to press many weeks before they appear in the bookshops and are inevitably out of date before publication day.

A paragraph of cold text detailing the content of a magazine can never convey the style and flavour of that particular publication. All it can do is give an indication of the type of material the magazine uses and those requirements can change both quickly and dramatically. So use these handbooks by all means, but never use them as a substitute for studying the magazine itself.

A better way to keep bang up to date with market information – and keep in touch with other writers – is by subscribing to a magazine like *Writers News*. As well as a whole range of practical features on different aspects of writing for publication, *Writers News* contains the latest details of market opportunities and editorial requirements. Make just one sale and the annual subscription has more than paid for itself.

The comprehensive Newscast section at the front of the magazine contains information and contact addresses for the latest competitions, magazine launches and policy changes. At the back of the magazine lies my own Market Index feature which, each month, dissects the market for a particular type of magazine.

Over the years Market Index has covered everything from pony magazines to photographic publications, sports titles to stamp collecting. Editors tell us what they want – and do not want – from contributors and we regularly revisit the most popular markets to make sure readers are kept right up to date.

There have been a number of marked changes in the style and approach of many mainstream publications over the last few years. Many major new titles have established themselves, some from overseas publishers, whilst others have amalgamated or folded altogether. Most have lost circulation in the face of economic recession and all are constantly striving for more sales by regularly adopting a 'new look' to an old friend.

Most editors are being told to cut costs, which unfortunately means that more material is being generated in-house or commissioned out to regular freelance contributors against a tight budget. The pool of freelance writers has also grown as magazines cut their salaried staff, making competition even tougher.

So good solid market study is all the more important if you want to sell your work in today's climate. Study your target publication carefully – not just one issue, but as many as you can find – until you know exactly what makes that magazine tick.

But changes are not just taking place behind the scenes of the British publishing industry. Many are much more upfront and significantly affect the type of copy required from journalists.

Undoubtedly the greatest trend has been to what are popularly known as 'bite-sized chunks'. Many of the biggest circulation women's magazines have moved towards shorter articles with lots of snippets to break up the printed page. Not only are articles shrinking in size, they are also dwindling in number. There is less to read and more to look at. Pictures have become much more important, both to support the editorial and to stand alone.

So what does this mean for the writer? It means that there is far less scope for in-depth features, except with some of the more upmarket glossy magazines which still pride themselves on a good read. Specialist titles in the how-to and hobby fields still contain a good number of lengthy articles, but pictures are important to them too, especially amongst competitive bookstall titles such as the riding and interior design magazines.

Gone are the days of writing 'as much as it will make'. Time was when a good journalist would be given rein to write as much – or as little – as he or she felt the subject merited. Nowadays, 1,500 words is a long article. Writing therefore needs to be tight if you are to make your words work for you.

This new trend does mean however that there is room for more individual contributions to many mainstream titles. And because they are shorter, they generally do not take so long to research and write – although this does not mean you should take any less care. In fact you may need to take even more care. Rates of pay, especially from the overseas publishers, are high and competition is strong.

On the plus side, a lot of new magazines have been launched in recent years, especially in the specialist areas of hobbies and activities. So instead of a few general magazines about caravanning, for example, there is now a full range of enthusiast – or 'niche' titles – covering everything from touring caravans through motor caravans to mobile homes.

Most subject areas are similarly subdivided, creating a wide range of opportunities for the knowledgeable freelance. And – even better news as far as the novice writer is concerned – many of them are prepared to work your writing into shape so long as the content is original, inspiring and accurate.

So even if you are already established in one or more market areas, you should always be on the lookout for new openings. A few hours spent on some thorough market study might turn up a new market with a similar kind of title or an opportunity to write for something entirely different. And what journalist can resist that challenge... ?

STARTING POINTS

If this is your first attempt at getting into print, you would do well to cut your literary teeth in a market where competition is not so hot and editors have time to encourage new talent. Not that the big nationals do not want to – they just have no need to. There are plenty of writers willing and able to produce the quality copy they require. And although some magazines do have a large support team, many publish with surprisingly few editorial staff, which all adds up to a pretty hectic operation.

Far better then to gain experience and confidence in some of the less competitive areas. They may offer lower rates of pay, but when you are just starting out and anxious for sales and experience, it is well worth swallowing your pride and aiming your sights a little lower. County magazines are often a good market for novice writers, as are some of the smaller circulation hobby titles.

Start by writing about what you know. Once you have notched up a few small successes in areas you know well, you will be better equipped to research and write about new topics.

When you are researching potential markets, look out for magazines which actually invite readers to contribute. Several women's magazines run a reader's own page, usually along some kind of theme – a day to remember, the holiday of a lifetime, my childhood memories, and so on.

Look too for articles and fillers which are obviously

provided by readers – how I built my model railway layout, the day my baby was born, household hints my mother gave me – not forgetting the letters page.

Readers' letters can actually prove a modest but steady source of income. Consider for a moment how many different publications you could submit to – any number of general interest women's titles (yes, even if you are a man), one or more magazines catering for your particular hobby or activity, your local county publication, and perhaps a business or trade journal.

With a little thought there is no reason why you should not write several letters a week – fewer words in total than an average article but with a very respectable earning potential. If you get £5 for a 50-word letter, that is equivalent to £100 for a 1,000-word article. Many national titles pay more, with perhaps £20 or £30 for the Star Letter or a valuable prize.

Competitions can also be a good starting point. Many writers' groups open their competitions to external entrants on payment of a small fee. Others – often with large cash prizes – are run by a variety of literary societies and commercial organisations. Watch for details in *Writers News*.

Make sure you read the rules carefully. Pay careful attention to the subject matter and any restrictions on eligibility. You do not want to waste time entering a competition for Yorkshire writers if you are living in Lancashire.

But whichever market you aim at, it is vital you study it thoroughly before you start. Otherwise you risk spending time and effort producing work which is totally unsuitable for the magazine's readership. Market study can only save you time in the long run, so make sure you know how to go about it.

And if you are already selling your work, it is well worth reassessing your market research methods. Many of us get sloppy as we become more confident in our abilities and fail to study the potential of new markets properly.

ANALYSING A PUBLICATION

Start by looking at a group of magazines. At first glance, they may all seem to cater for the same reader. But a closer look will reveal that they are aimed at different age groups, social groups and, in the case of hobby or specialist titles, different levels of interest or expertise.

Take motoring magazines, for example. As well as titles for the general auto enthusiast, there are specialist publications aimed at custom car owners, sports car drivers, rally competitors, amateur mechanics, and classic car drivers.

The same sort of split can be seen amongst any general category. Some, of course, are more obvious than others. The title alone will be indicative of the contents. Others – notably the women's press – can be more difficult to pigeonhole. The differences between say *Woman, Woman's Own, Woman's Realm* and *Woman's Weekly* will not become apparent until you sit down and study them carefully.

Do your market research thoroughly and it is surprising just how much you can learn about the way a magazine ticks. But never be tempted to study just one issue. Ideally you should read at least three or four before you start work on your own submission.

So what is the best way to go about it? There are three things to bear in mind when studying any publication – the target reader, the style of writing and the openings for freelances.

(1) The Reader

Before you plunge into the inside pages, take time to study the cover. After all, that is the page which is designed to attract the buyers. Study the cover shot. Does it relate to a main feature or is it merely a pretty picture? If the magazine is a woman's title, what sort of cover girl do they use?

A line on the spine – or perhaps under the main title – may tell you something about the approach of the magazine. 'Better food. Better homes. Better living.' 'Real issues, real interest'. 'The magazine for women who juggle their lives'. 'Practical advice for owners and riders'. 'Designing, building and extending your home'. All summaries of the magazine's contents.

Look carefully at the cover lines which highlight that issue's main features. A magazine which promises 'Step-by-step to meals in moments' plus 'A jolly jester doll to knit' is aiming for a different reader from the one which teases with 'Madly in love – the pain and horror of obsession' and 'Ten classic career mistakes women always make'.

A magazine's advertisements will tell you a lot about its readers. Company advertising agencies spend a lot of time and money researching the people they want to reach. So let them do your work for you.

A magazine which advertises children's toys, clothes and cough mixtures, alongside perfume, cosmetics and hairsprays is obviously aimed primarily at the woman with a young family. Very different from the publication which advertises stairlifts, commodes and thermal underwear.

Similarly, a glossy publication which carries adverts for sports cars and exotic holidays targets a different economic group from the one which advertises family saloons and budget breaks in Britain.

Look down the contents page and examine the balance of features. What sort of subjects do they cover? Is there emphasis on one particular type of feature or are there perhaps two or three areas with equal weight? You will need to read them all in due course, but a preliminary look should be enough to start building up a picture of that target reader.

The letters page should reinforce that. Do readers write in response to articles in previous issues? Do they use the letters page as a discussion forum for general issues related to the magazine's area of interest or do they simply send amusing anecdotes and helpful tips?

If the magazine has a problem page study that too. You will quickly be able to tell the age of the readers, the type of lives they lead and the level of information they require. Buyer's guides can also be helpful. The products featured have all been chosen because they will appeal to the readers.

But a word of warning about fashion pages in the women's press. Although a spread on mail order or chain store clothes will certainly be aimed at a less affluent readership, fashion pages are notorious purveyors of dreams. Even the glossies are sometimes criticised for their extravagance. So just remember that many garments will be featured for their inspirational value – and for the fact that they look good on the printed page.

(2) The Style

Once you have worked out who your target publication is aimed at, you need to study the style in which it is written. Is it chatty and informal with lots of short snappy articles? Does it take a more formal tone with longer, in-depth features? Or is it perhaps very practical with lots of solid 'how to' information?

Remember that if you are to stand any chance of success with that magazine, you will have to reproduce that house style in your own work. Your own individual style is of little consequence at this stage. What the editor wants is something which will slot easily in amongst the other copy, with minimal rewriting by his editorial team.

Wait till you get offered a regular column before stamping your own style too heavily on your work. The successful article writer is able to vary his style according to the publication he is writing for – a woman's title one day, a hobby magazine the next, and so on.

Look first at the overall length of each item. Some of course will be short fillers, others full-length features, but nevertheless a pattern should soon emerge. The editor knows his reader's attention span. He knows how many words he can allow for a discussion feature, a personality profile and a practical article.

There is no need to count every single word of each feature. Count up a typical column inch, multiply it by the number of inches in the column, and then by the number of columns. The result will give you a rough overall word count.

You may have to make slight adjustments up or down. Take this extract from a diet feature, for example, reproduced as it appeared in a women's magazine:

> * Remember there are even
>   low-fat crisps and low calorie
>   beers, wines and chocolates.
>   Cut right down on or cut out

if you can:
. chocolate or sweets
. pastry
. cakes and biscuits
. croissants
. cream

On the printed page, this section of text took up around one-and a half inches, yet it contained only 33 words. The same space in the main body of text contained around 70 words. But you will soon get a feel for the average space allotted to different types of article within a magazine – perhaps 1,500 or 2,000 words for a main feature, 1,000 for a one-pager, and a hundred or two for a filler.

Then look at the way those words are broken up into paragraphs. Are the paragraphs long or short, of similar or varying lengths? Is all the information contained in the main body of text or does the magazine make use of factboxes or footnotes?

Many consumer titles which specialise in practical features like to list key points or step-by-step instructions in separate boxes – or sidebars – often tinted in a different colour. They are visually eye-catching and easy for the reader to assimilate.

Similarly, an information box at the foot of an article can contain all the essential bits of information which may hold up the flow of an article if included in the main text. Travel articles, for example, are incomplete without an indication of price, how to get there and who can organise it. A brief footnote to the feature can include all these vital details without interrupting the writer's impressions and experiences. Some magazines also include sightseeing information and a 'best buy' guide at this point on the page.

Boxes are also sometimes used to highlight a piece of text relating to – but not included in – the main feature. For example, an article in a parentcraft magazine about working mothers may discuss childcare options in the body of the text and illustrate them by boxing off personal experience stories by working mothers. Again, this method is visually attractive and makes the article easier to read. It also makes it easier to write.

Study carefully the sentence construction and vocabulary. Does the magazine aim for maximum clarity and an easy read or is it aimed at a more intellectually demanding readership? Are the sentences short and simple, the vocabulary everyday? Or are the sentences longer and more complex?

Some magazines – especially amongst the hobby and specialist titles – produce editorial guidelines or 'tip sheets' which are designed to help the potential contributor. It is well worth a call to the editorial desk to ask if your target market offers such valuable information, free on receipt of an sae.

If they do, it not only helps with your homework, it also indicates that they encourage freelance contributors. If they do not have a tip sheet, they may nevertheless be able to offer some off the cuff tips over the phone. So have a few questions ready, just in case.

Once you have got the feel of the whole magazine, the balance between features and fillers, fact and fiction, take a closer look at the particular slot you hope to fill. Using the same criteria for length, style and structure, analyse the articles in depth. The less rewriting a sub-editor needs to do on your work, the more chance you will stand of selling to that publication again.

(3) Freelance Opportunities

Once you begin to understand who the readers of a magazine are and the style in which that magazine is written, you will want to know just what opportunities there might be for freelances. This is the tricky bit. There are ways you can get an idea, but unfortunately they are not infallible. Still, you can at least make a start.

Look first at the staff box, which is usually to be found at the beginning of the editorial pages. Sometimes this means on the first inside spread. Sometimes it may not appear until well into the magazine after pages of advertisements. It may be located deep inside on the letters page or even at the foot of the inside back page.

Wherever you find it, this list of personnel will show you whether the magazine has a big staff and whether it has separate editors for specific subjects. It will not, unfortunately, tell you how many of these staff are on the payroll.

A glossy monthly may, for example, have a travel editor, a cookery editor, a wine editor and a gardening editor, but they are unlikely to be on the permanent full-time staff. More likely, they are freelances who are retained as consulting editors, probably working from home and submitting their copy to a monthly deadline just like any other freelance.

But you can fairly safely assume that key supporting roles such as features and, where appropriate, fiction editors will be permanent fixtures of the editorial office. The information box may even list a direct line phone number by which to contact them.

Then go through the magazine – which you should be getting to know quite well by now – and compare the names on the articles with the names which appear in the editorial box. How many features are in fact written by staff writers? Often not many.

Study of a few consecutive issues will soon reveal whether things like wine, food and travel are written by that retained editor or whether the magazine accepts pieces from other writers on that topic too. You should also watch for other contributors whose names crop up in more than one issue. This indicates that the magazine uses a stable of regular outsiders. What you can not tell is whether or not you might have a chance of joining them.

Look for those pages which invite readers to contribute and, if you have something that fits the bill, send it in, paying careful attention to style and length. Hopefully your writing ability will make it stand out from the average reader contribution.

But do not send it in without enclosing a couple of other ideas that you could contribute elsewhere in the magazine. If they like your style – and your ideas – you might just be asked to send them in on spec.

MARKET INFORMATION ON TAP

Market research takes time, though hopefully you will find it enjoyable as well as useful. So do not let the information go to waste. Out of six magazines you research thoroughly now, you may only have ideas to suit one of them, but that does not mean your efforts have been wasted. Not only will you understand where that title fits in amongst its competitors, you will also have in-depth knowledge of those other titles for the moment when inspiration strikes.

A card index system or ringbinder is the most flexible way to store market data. Magazines can change with surprising frequency. Sometimes the changes are dramatic – a total relaunch – but most of the time they are more subtle. A new column. A change to an old one. Whatever the change, you want to be aware of it and adapt your writing to suit it.

It may be, for example, that a general interest magazine has changed from doing a full-blown personality profile to a celebrity snippet page. It may have stopped taking fiction or started taking poetry. Your favourite hobby magazine may have started a reader's experience page or your county magazine may be running a series on local churchyards. Old news is no news, so you need to keep your market research system bang up to date.

Card indexes are easily updated with changes of addresses, phone number or editorial personnel, but the cards are small, which means they are not so easy for recording detailed market information or for including examples.

You might therefore like to supplement your index box by using a ringbinder to store up to date examples of various types of features from different magazines – cross-referenced into your card system of course. This method saves storing whole magazines and provides a ready reference if an idea breaks after the newsagent has closed for the weekend.

AIM OF THE FREELANCE

When you first start writing for publication, write anything you think you can place. It will give you practice in analysing markets, practice in writing, and – if you sell – an unprecedented boost to your ego. But as you become more established, it is a good idea to settle yourself into a handful of markets you feel comfortable with.

This means finding editors who like your work and who buy most – ideally all – of what you send them. After a while, the natural progression from this is that they give you work, which cuts down on the time you spend finding ideas. They may also give you contacts as well, which cuts down on research.

It pays to find editors – or publishers – who pay promptly. In these tight economic times, a publisher who pays on acceptance is worth many times more than the one who pays after publication. You might wait a year for publication and more than that for your money.

Similarly, find editors who are good to deal with. It is not essential, but it certainly helps if you can find an editor who is on the same wavelength. Physical distance may mean that you never actually meet face to face, but if he is only a phone call away when you have a query or a problem, you will enjoy a far more relaxed working relationship. And what writer needs hassle?

But even if you are lucky enough to establish yourself in three or four different markets, never shut eyes to new openings. Today's freelances need to be flexible in their approach if they are to keep working. Keep you eyes open for new magazines, new opportunities within old ones, and new areas that you could contribute to.

Specialists are all very well until suddenly their speciality is not needed any more, so try and gain as broad a writing experience as possible and be prepared to turn your hand to anything. Work on the basis of 'Have notebook, will travel' and you are unlikely to waste any opportunity to improve your output – and your reputation.

4
RESEARCH

THE FAMILIAR AND THE UNFAMILIAR

If this is your first attempt at writing for publication, your best hope of getting into print is to write about something you know. Your own experiences and interests should provide you with a ready source of ideas. They are also easiest to research.

You may have enough knowledge to write one or more articles without any additional research at all. Your hobby, your job or some other aspect of your daily life. If not, you could well have sufficient material at home to enable you to do your research 'in house' – handbooks or specialist magazines, for instance.

You will almost certainly know where to go for further information. The type of books to look for at the library, for example, or the whereabouts of a relevant club or association. Perhaps you are already a member. You should also be familiar with a few potential markets, magazines which are either devoted to or regularly interested in articles on your chosen subject.

Writing about what you know is like meeting up with an old friend. Comfortable, undemanding, but ultimately unchallenging. Just as sooner or later, we all need the stimulus of new friends, so the serious writer will want to seek new ideas and new markets. All of which means writing about subjects you do not know.

When you first branch out into unknown territory, you will probably feel unsure of yourself. Where should you go for information? How easy will it be to find? And of course will you understand it once you have found it? But once you gain in experience, you will also gain in confidence. Soon you will be able to tackle almost any subject.

If a market opportunity presents itself, grab it with both hands. Magazines may be tightening up, but there are still plenty of opportunities – if you are not afraid to accept a challenge. And who knows, you may find it is not as terrifying as you think.

A chance conversation with the editor of a home interest magazine, for example, might reveal an opening for a writer who can provide property profiles. This particular editor puts greater store on good contacts and interview skills, rather than interior design experience. The readership is not highly specialised so the writer simply needs to be able to ask the sort of questions that readers would want answered.

Nevertheless, you will need to do some background research first if you hope to sell your piece. Read through several back copies of the target publication, as well as some competitive titles. Take note of the style and approach of similar features and try to familiarise yourself with any jargon. You could even get some ideas from a local designer or furnishing store.

Then you are away. If you sell that first piece and are able to come up with some more feature ideas, you may find yourself with a new and regular market. And the more features you do, the more at ease you will be with the subject. A real case of learning on the job.

Some articles, however, will require more extensive research – books from a specialised library, for instance, information from a national association or governing body, or perhaps an interview with an expert. This does not have to be very difficult and it can be tremendous fun, so long as you understand a few basic points about researching:

– Have an idea of what you want before you start. Whether you are looking for material at your local library or asking an organisation for help, you will progress much faster if you can be specific with your questions or requests for literature.

– Never waste any material. It might not be needed for this article, but could come in useful for a follow-up. You may even find it throws up another idea you can write now for a different market.

– Remember to double check everything you read in a book or magazine. Just because it is in print, does not mean it is accurate. Read two or three different newspaper accounts of the same story and you will invariably find at least one discrepancy in the reports. And of course subsequent events may turn the whole story on its head. So never risk perpetuating mistakes and losing credibility with your editor or readers. Check and recheck whenever possible.

– Do not forget that research can be addictive. Some writers get so absorbed that they put off the process of actually writing up their finds. So discipline yourself and do not forget why you are researching in the first place.

– Research can be very time consuming and expensive too, especially if you need to travel to far flung information sources. We all want to sell our work, but unless you are passionately committed to writing a particular article, it is worth weighing up whether the time spent accumulating material is going to be worth it in terms of payment or prestige. You may well be able to put your time to better – and more profitable – use.

BUILDING UP YOUR OWN LIBRARY

All writers need their own library. No, not the one in the high street, but a home ready reference section they can consult at a moment's notice. You cannot, of course, stock everything you might be likely to need, but some well chosen books and other reference material should fulfil most of your everyday needs and can often provide leads that can be followed up over the telephone.

Cuttings

Storage and retrieval problems make it impossible for most

writers to keep magazines and newspapers on file, but a good cuttings library is easy to maintain and an invaluable source of background information.

It is also highly personalised. You can collect cuttings on subjects which interest you, divided and sub-divided to suit your own individual way of working. You can use large envelopes or cardboard folders, see-through wallets or even supermarket boxes. They are inexpensive and easy to store, either near your work space or in the bottom of a cupboard.

I keep my cuttings in box files, divided by general subject and then again into specific topics. At the moment I have four files on Celebrities, two on Travel, two on Family and Childcare, one on Horses, a Local box and a large one labelled Miscellaneous.

The celebrity files are further sub-divided. Two of them, headed 'Celebrities – by file', contain plastic wallets of cuttings on high profile personalities. Some are people I have interviewed before and may want to interview again; others are people I hope one day to meet.

The other two are simply labelled 'Celebrities – miscellaneous'. Here I put one-off cuttings about people in the news, perhaps television or sports personalities who may form the subject of a marketable feature. If I collect more than a couple of cuttings on one person, I give them their own plastic wallet and transfer them to the 'Celebrities – by file' boxes. Status indeed!

The drawback with my system is that I have to thumb through all the individual cuttings or plastic folders to find the one I am looking for. They would be easier to find – but more time-consuming to file – if I arranged them alphabetically or kept an index.

However the upside – and this, to me, is more important – is that by making retrieval just that little more difficult, I am frequently browsing through the whole box. It actually takes only minutes, but it has often revealed forgotten information relating to someone who has suddenly become marketable.

My Travel files contain mostly brochures and leaflets from places of interest – regional tourist guides, leaflets on days out, stately homes, theme parks, and so on. Most of these are free from UK and overseas tourist boards and are useful not only for writers of travel articles but also for much broader purposes.

So if I were preparing an article, for example, on theme parks for a consumer magazine, a feature on steam trains for a railway magazine, or a discussion piece on our vanishing coastline for an environmental publication, I should find plenty of leads in my Travel files. Most travel literature is updated every year, so do not forget to get hold of the latest copies.

The file labelled Horses contains a variety of articles about riding personalities, leaflets from equestrian organisations, and jottings of useful addresses and phone numbers. Any hobbyist could compile a similar file around his own interest.

Family and Childcare relates to just that – cuttings from national papers and parentcraft magazines about various aspects of childcare and child development. I am not a specialist so I tend to avoid anything too learned or experimental, but I am a mother and am always interested in the mum's viewpoint.

So into the file goes anything which I think might make the basis of a feature for mums like me. And that means everything from where to take tots for a cheap day out to coping with school lunches, how to enforce discipline to teaching your child about wildlife.

My Local file, as might be expected, includes anything of local interest, such as details of organisations, newspaper cuttings, and literature on places of interest. Personalities are cross-referenced to the Celebrity files; places to the Travel file; and so on. Many of them have gone on to become the subject of a national magazine article.

Finally there is the Miscellaneous file. This mostly contains booklets and brochures which do not automatically fall into any of my favourite subject areas but look too helpful to throw away. Which leads to another principle of researching – if in doubt, do not throw out. You are bound to regret it afterwards.

Get into the habit of collecting cuttings and you will soon build up a useful reference library. Never throw a publication away without scanning it for useful information. It only takes a few minutes, but it is time well spent. Ask your friends and family to save old magazines and papers for you and do not forget to look through those in public waiting rooms. If you spot something useful, a quiet word with the receptionist will probably end with you taking the magazine home with you – or at least tearing out the relevant page, without feeling guilty about it.

Books

Books are expensive so you will need to be selective about which ones you buy rather than borrow. And nice though it is to see well stocked shelves around the home, the working writer really only needs a few basic works. The others can easily be borrowed or consulted at your local library.

There are often bargains to be had on the secondhand bookstalls. Obviously information which does not date is your best buy, but it is still worth scooping up last year's almanac or yearbook. It may help to get you started on a particular project and the information can always be brought up to date at your local library.

So which books do you really need? Some kind of writer's directory is essential. The *Writers' & Artists' Yearbook* is a popular choice, as is *The Writer's Handbook*. Both are published annually and carry details of a wide range of magazines, as well as book publishers, agents, and so on.

Some writers maintain that you should replace your chosen annual every year, but alternate years is probably soon enough. The entries inevitably date very quickly and no experienced writer would dream of submitting work to a title purely on the strength of a short paragraph in a directory. Detailed market study is essential.

A good dictionary and a one volume encyclopedia are essential. It is important to find a book you feel comfortable with. So take time in the library or local bookshop to find your way around the different volumes and buy the ones that best suit your needs – and your budget.

Some writers swear by a thesaurus, though if you are

working for consumer titles you may find it is rarely used. What you need are words which easily spring to mind. However it is certainly a useful volume to have and a paperback version should be sufficient for most article writers.

A book on English usage – both words and punctuation – is also a good buy, but do buy carefully. Some are more palatable than others and certainly more practical. Choose one that you had be happy to keep by your bedside – one which is interesting to read as well as clearly set out.

You are more likely to learn good grammar by browsing through it for pleasure than consulting it to solve a specific problem – presuming, of course, that you realise you have even got a problem! So it is no good buying a learned tome, if you never feel tempted to look at it.

Two useful – and enjoyable – volumes are *Write Right!* by Jan Venolia and *The Penguin Dictionary of Troublesome Words* by Bill Bryson. *Usage and Abusage* by Eric Partridge and *The Complete Plain Words* by Sir Ernest Gowers are also popular, if a trifle more literary.

Another good buy is a dictionary of dates such as *Harrap's Book of British Dates* – excellent inspiration for anniversary articles as well as a valuable source of useful snippets to drop casually into your copy.

Finally, buy anything that interests you and does not burst the book budget – a definitive handbook to your hobby, for example, a book of quotations or specialist publication. If you know that you will use it, it is worth the money. And after all, if it brings in just one sale, it will more than have paid for itself.

As for anything else, borrow it, but do learn to make the most of your local library first. Many writers do not realise the wealth of information that is available on their doorstep, most of it free of charge. Libraries can provide many useful contacts and information sources, as well as a vast range of books and periodicals.

USING YOUR LOCAL LIBRARY

It sounds like an obvious question, but do you actually know everything your library has to offer? You could be surprised. The library facilities on your doorstep will depend, to a large extent, on where you live. If you live in a rural area, for example, you may have a small selection of books brought to your door by a mobile library. Whilst the borrower who lives in a London borough or other major city, may be able to walk from one big library to another.

The International Federation of Library Associations (IFLA) lays down standards regarding the size of libraries per thousand head of population, as well as the book stock they carry, but these are often difficult to enforce. A large town may demand a bigger library than the small town down the road, but it all comes down to the availability of both land and public money.

Yet although libraries vary vastly in the book stock they carry, they should all be able to offer a comparable service. And for the writer, it is well worth spending time getting to know that service.

Best place to start is at the Information desk. Library staff are highly trained and at your service, so make use of them. They are also very busy, so help them to help you by remembering a few basic rules:

– Introduce yourself to the staff and find out which are quiet times if you are going to be needing assistance. The library service has to be egalitarian and offer everyone the same service, so it is in your interest to try and ask questions at a time when the staff are not too busy.

– Be specific. Do not just ask for the section on domestic pets if what you want is a book on grooming poodles. Tell the assistant exactly what sort of information you are after, how much information you have already, and which publications – if any – you have already read. This avoids both duplication of effort and going off at the wrong tangent.

– Have patience. Answers cannot always be immediate. It may take time to track down the book or information you want. It may have to come from another library. But remember that if all you leave with is a telephone number of someone to contact, you are one step further forward with your project.

– Be realistic. Your local library is not a research institution. There may be plenty of willingness but there will almost certainly be a shortage of time and resources. So do not expect them to do all your work for you. Library staff will be happy to gather material ready for collection but it is up to you to check that it is what you want.

– Similarly, it is quite acceptable to phone through an enquiry for a single piece of information you need for an article – a date perhaps or a name and address – but do not expect the staff to provide a whole list of answers for you.

The library assistant may refer you to the catalogue for the name and reference number of a specific title. More and more libraries are going over from the old card index system to computer terminals. These are fast, efficient and easy to use, but do not be afraid to ask for a demonstration if this is your first attempt. You may be able to access the catalogues of other libraries in the area as well as your own.

Computer terminals may also be used for storing newspaper and magazine indexes, not just to the archives of that particular branch, but often to those of the whole county library service. Most large libraries keep back copies of *The Times* and some may also stock other national papers, as well as local titles.

They may also keep indexes to popular magazines which may be used as sources of reference – titles such as *Good Housekeeping*, *Country Life* and the *Scientific American*, for example. Your library should also have access to on-line databases which can draw on a variety of sources worldwide.

It may also be able to point you in the right direction via its stock of telephone directories. A large library will usually stock directories for its own catchment area, whilst a major library may stock them for the whole county, either on fiche or in hardback edition.

The public library service is basically free to those living in the area, but there is usually a small charge for certain specific items such as reservations and recordings. There is no additional charge for obtaining material on inter-library loan, even though this can cost several pounds in time and administrative costs. If a requested item is going to be very expensive to locate, you may be asked if it is, in fact, essential. You will not, however, be asked to pay the cost.

Specialisations

Major libraries within each county often specialise in particular types of books. They decide which collections they want to enhance their own local community and then become the local centre for that particular subject.

So one library, for example, may specialise in history and geography, whilst another focusses on science and technology, music and drama, or perhaps the fine arts. These special collections are housed within that one county centre but available to borrowers anywhere in the area on inter-county loan.

If you still cannot find what you want from the public libraries, your local library has access to college libraries within the county. You may be able to borrow books for study at home or, if the book is retained in the reference section, be permitted access to the college library on a reader's ticket.

Still drawn a blank? Do not despair. Information on sibling rivalry requested from a mobile village library yielded photocopies of studies held at the private library of a child development institution. And all for the cost of the photocopies, which the writer was subsequently allowed to keep.

If you are planning to write articles on a particular topic, ask about any specialisations within your county library service before you start. You might be surprised at the range of information at your disposal.

For example, a library specialising in Health Information will have an enormous collection on matters medical and paramedical. As well as a variety of leaflets and other literature, the library will probably stock relevant publications such as *Nursing Times* and *The Lancet*, which may be required for reference. It will also have access to a wide variety of private medical libraries.

Similarly, a library which specialises in local history will carry a lot more than just books about the area. As well as census returns and other local records, it may hold a surprisingly varied collection of ephemera which has been donated by local residents and organisations.

County records are kept in the County Records Office, which holds a wide range of documents relating to the history and administration of the county. These will include parish registers and other ecclesiastical records, maps, family and business archives, as well as official records of local government, schools and so on. You will also find a range of maps and town plans – old and new – and probably photographs, prints and paintings.

Entry is generally via a Readers' Ticket, which simply means that you must give your name and address and produce some form of identification before being admitted to the collection. You may need to reserve a microfilm reader or give advance notice if you wish to consult some particularly delicate or cumbersome document, so it is well worth phoning up to make an appointment. There are generally no fees to pay for using the County Records Office, except for instances where a fee is required by law.

In addition to the Public Library Service, there are other specialist libraries which can be used by the general public, either as members or on a readers ticket. One of the most famous of these is the British Library Newspaper Library in North London, which stocks UK national and regional newspapers dating back to the 18th century, as well as many foreign titles. Ask at your local library for details of this and other specialist collections.

Useful Volumes

There are all kinds of unexpected aids for the article writer lurking on the library shelves – if only you know what to look for. The following titles should prove useful:

- *Directory of British Associations*
  From Action Against Allergy to the Zoological Society of London, this indispensable directory lists associations both alphabetically and by subject matter. Whatever you are researching, you are sure to find at least one organisation that can help you. 'Mice', for example, have one entry, 'wallcoverings' have three, and 'roses', five; but there are seventeen entries under 'plants' and twenty under 'food'.

- *ASLIB Directory of Information Sources in the UK*
  Smaller libraries may not stock this two-volume work which lists hundreds of specialist organisations which have their own libraries or information centres. However your local branch may be able to access the information you need.

- *Willings Press Guide*
  All the publications you ever dreamed about and more are listed in this annual guide to the world's periodicals. Volume 1 covers the UK, whilst Volume 2 deals with overseas. Listed alphabetically and by subject, each entry includes a brief summary of content and target readership as well as advertising rates and production data.

- *Whitaker's Almanac*
  Almost a British institution, Whitaker's Almanac celebrates its 125th edition in 1993. It boasts the broadest range of information in any one volume reference book and covers everything from armed forces to currencies, local government through world statistics.

- *Who's Who*
  Another legendary but often overlooked source of information for the article writer. Many of the 28,000 individuals whose biographies appear in the current edition are of interest to the professional interviewer. They come from

all walks of life and include many popular showbusiness personalities – Terry Wogan is just one – as well as academics and public figures. Contact addresses just might provide that vital lead you have been looking for.

Efficient Notetaking

Do make sure that you make the most of the information on offer by making sufficiently detailed notes. You do not want to make a return trip just to check a date, a spelling or some other snippet of information, especially if the library is some distance away.

Take plenty of paper with you and do not be afraid to use it. A clean sheet for each item will enable you to file your information neatly when you get home. And write on side of the paper only, otherwise you will find yourself having to write half of it out again.

Annotate each piece of information carefully. Which book or paper it came from, which library you found it in... even the location of the book on the shelf. You never know when you might need it again. Date each sheet and double check all dates and spellings. One figure or letter out of place and your credibility takes an instant nose dive.

NATIONAL ORGANISATIONS AND COMMERCIAL COMPANIES

A browse through the Directory of British Associations, will reveal that there is an organisation or association for almost everything. Often several. What you may not know is that they can often do a large part of your research for you, at least as far as providing material is concerned.

You are looking for experts. The experts are invariably looking for publicity, whether they are a charity or pressure group trying to promote their campaign, a commercial company hoping to push their products, or a government department wishing to publicise their work. Add to this trade associations and unions, tourist boards and embassies, and you soon find you have a whole range of experts available for the asking.

So how does it all work? Most organisations employ someone to handle promotional activities. In a small outfit, this may be a single person who combines publicity work with some other function such as sales or marketing.

It may – in the case of an international company, a television network or a government department – involve a whole department with several people each looking after a particular aspect of the organisation's activities. Or they may buy in the services of a public relations agency to organise promotions, produce literature and generally handle enquiries from outside.

How you approach them is up to you. Some writers devise a questionnaire if they are contacting more than one company, but these are often treated like circulars – tucked in the bottom of the in-tray for that spare moment that never comes.

You can of course write a letter, but letters too get lost in the pile. A telephone call is far more direct and enables you to pursue another line of enquiry immediately if your first effort draws a blank. The *Writers' & Artists' Yearbook* lists government offices and public services in the UK, as well as television companies and radio stations. British Telecom's Directory Enquiries service can also be of help.

Not only will a telephone call save you time, it will also be more specific. You may think you require a particular piece or type of information, but when you actually speak to someone in the know, you often find that there are different aspects to your query, that more information is available if you want it, or that another department or organisation could help you even further.

So once you have got the telephone number, simply call the switchboard and ask for the press or public relations department. Some organisations have both. Some have one or the other. Explain who you are, what sort of piece you are writing and the kind of information you want. If they are halfway professional, they will know how to do the rest.

Remember that they need your help as much as you need theirs. You should therefore be dealt with politely and promptly. You should also find that most of the information they provide will come free of charge.

So what sort of material can you ask for? A lot depends, of course on the type of organisation you are dealing with. A commercial company, for example, will have product leaflets, annual reports, technical information and sales figures. A charity may have case history studies, statistical information, and campaign literature, whilst a tourist board will have leaflets on where to go, what to see and where to stay.

In fact you will invariably find you end up with too much material. But do not waste it. You may be able to write a second piece from a different angle for another publication. If not now, almost certainly later. So add it to your personal research library and, if necessary, create a new file for it.

In addition to printed material, a press or PR office should also be able to provide you with people – an expert to interview or a guided tour to help with your research. So brush up your interview techniques with the help of Chapter 9 and see whose expertise you can call on.

An efficient press office will also be able to arrange to have your copy checked. Never submit any manuscript with a technical or medical content to an editor without first having it checked by the experts. However well you think you have understood the leaflets – or the interview – it is frighteningly easy to misinterpret information, to take something out of context or be too economical with your explanations.

So make sure you complete the copy ahead of deadline, leaving time to have your finished article checked. If you cut corners and the editor receives complaints that your article is inaccurate, he will not be buying your work again. Nor will you find the offended organisation so helpful next time round.

CULTIVATING CONTACTS

Once you have made a contact at a particular organisation, use it. That is not being manipulative, it is simply being practical. Start by asking to go on the mailing list. Most organisations send out regular news stories – called press releases –

to selected publications and freelances, so make sure you are one of them.

A short news story can often be turned into a full-length feature taken in a broader context. Even if you can not see a market for it straightaway, it is worth putting away in a file dedicated to that organisation. You do not know what may happen next week and how you may wish you had kept it.

A short item may spark off an idea which will need you to contact other similar – perhaps competitive – organisations. A product feature, for example, such as washing powders, garden furniture or children's toys. If you do use information from a variety of sources, remember to keep a balance. You may be sent loads of free samples from one particular manufacturer, but do not let this become apparent in the way your present your comparisons. And remember, press releases are meant to glow with enthusiasm – you do not have to.

If you receive information from a public relations agency, ask who else they deal with. Whilst researching an article on windows and doors for an interior design magazine, I had to contact an agency for pictures of an innovative new design to illustrate the feature. The agency's main area of work was actually in sports promotion but they had two rather offbeat accounts – the window company and one of the country's foremost cathedral choir schools. The result was a double page spread in the Christmas issue of a national women's magazine about the boys who work at Christmas.

Publishers can be helpful too. A quick call to their press office is all it takes to get yourself a copy of their latest catalogue. Most of the authors will be available for interview and probably only too happy to help. Publicity budgets are usually limited to just a few top-selling authors so any opportunity to get further publicity in the shape of interviews and editorial is always welcome.

A nice perk of interviewing authors is that you do get a free copy of their latest book. Sometimes their previous ones as well. But do be fair. If you are sent a review copy out of the blue and can not find a market for a feature, that is the publisher's problem. However it is unethical to ask for copies unless you genuinely believe you can sell the idea to an editor.

You may end up with some nice books, but do it too often and you could find your source of books – and feature material – soon dries up.

Another perk about article writing is the variety of invitations you receive to press functions once you get known. Some are simply cocktail parties or buffets to promote a book or a product. Others involve visits to film studios, exhibitions, even holidays abroad.

As a freelance you are perfectly entitled to accept anything you are offered, but it is always worth trying to secure a commission before you go. It helps enormously with knowing what questions to ask or what information to gather, and it also does your credibility a power of good. Freelances do attend functions in the hope they can sell a piece afterwards, but you will go up in everyone's estimation if you can do it the other way round.

Keep all the names, addresses and phone numbers of your PR contacts in a dedicated address book or card index, including details of the type of work they do and other useful information. Every few weeks, skim through the names and, if you have not heard from someone for a while, contact them. People do 'fall off' address lists from time to time, but show you are seriously interested in article ideas and you will not be forgotten again. You may even get in first and steal a scoop.

PICTURE RESEARCH

The writer who can take his own photographs not only ensures he gets the right shots, he also stands to double his money. Thanks to today's sophisticated technology, you do not need to be an expert photographer to take saleable pictures.

Any automatic compact 35mm camera – coupled with a reasonable eye for composition – will enable you to illustrate your articles professionally. Read the camera instructions carefully and take a few test rolls before you attempt anything for publication.

Most of today's magazines prefer colour slides, but check

with the editorial office before you shoot. Your local photo dealer can advise you on choosing the right film, as well as how to get the best results from your camera.

There are, however, times when it is not practical to illustrate an article with your own photographs. So where else can you go for illustrations? Your local photographic club might be able to provide you with useful contacts, but if you ask anyone to take pictures for you, make sure it is clear whether you pay them out of your fee for the article or whether the magazine pays them direct.

There are plenty of commercial picture agencies listed in the *Writers' & Artist's Yearbook* who provide illustrations on all manner of subjects, but reproduction fees are high. There are a lot of free pictures available just for the asking – if you know where to look.

Any press or PR Office who can provide you with information and experts, should also be able to lend pictures. Companies, for example, usually keep a range of product shots on file. They can be rather bland, if the product is not particularly photogenic, but they may be willing to take new ones to accompany free editorial. After all, the costs of photography are small compared to the cost of buying advertising space.

Television companies are usually a much better bet when it comes to eye-catching photos. They can lend you stills from shows and should have a choice of colour or black and white, prints or transparencies, according to what your magazine prefers. Similarly, tourist boards usually have good stocks of attractive location shots to illustrate travel or environment features.

Charities often hold extensive picture libraries, though you may find the shots are not as professional as you would like. Many are taken for archive purposes rather than publication, though you may be able to borrow better quality stills from annual reports or publicity leaflets.

Finally, remember that you do not necessarily need photographs to illustrate an article. A local history piece, for instance, might call for line drawings, engravings, or maps. A company logo might feature in a business profile or a diagram in a technical article. You could even draw your own cartoon.

You should take every possible precaution to ensure that you do not infringe copyright by using someone else's illustration. In the case of an old photograph, for instance, the publishers of the book or magazine in which it first appears may be able to tell you who owns the copyright.

If the publisher bought the copyright, it remains his for 50 years, but if he bought only reproduction rights to the picture, the copyright remains with the photographer himself. It is then up to you to try and trace him or his descendants.

Should you draw a blank, it is worth taking legal advice on the advisability of reproducing the photograph. Copyright is a complex subject and it is not worth risking an expensive law suit. Find an alternative picture instead.

LOCAL SOCIETIES

Do not overlook the research opportunities on your doorstep. It is well worth spending a few minutes browsing amongst the notices in your local library for details of clubs, societies and support groups. Many local papers also publish regular lists of organisations, with names and telephone numbers of people to contact.

Many of these are local branches of national organisations and provide excellent feature opportunities. The chance to attend a meeting of the local branch of a national organisation for the parents of crying babies, was too good an opportunity to miss.

A group of around ten mothers met in the group leader's house for coffee and chatted readily about their experiences and feelings of desperation over a child who never stopped crying. Result? Three different articles – one for a general woman's magazine, one for a parentcraft title, and another for the local paper.

Local groups are also able to put you in contact with the national organisation, who in turn can provide literature, further contacts and often books or videos. So whether you are interested in hobbies or politics, self-help or support groups, do not forget the research possibilities close to home.

INFORMATION AT A PRICE

A great deal of information is free for the price of a phone call, a stamp or the time it takes you to track it down. However you can pay someone else to do it for you.

The Information Bureau, for example, is a London-based organisation which gives the busy journalist access to press cuttings, facts and statistics, political information, biographies and events on almost any subject you care to mention. But it costs you.

Formerly with the *Daily Telegraph*, the Information Bureau employs skilled researchers who have an extensive archive, database and reference library at their disposal. At the time of writing, charges – based on the amount of research time required – start at £20 for 15 minutes, £65 for an hour, or £15 and £20 respectively, if you first pay an annual subscription of £100.

If you are willing to pay the price, phone 071-924 4414 to discuss your budget, information requirements and deadline.

RESEARCH THROUGH FRIENDS

Many of your friends will find themselves – or their experiences – in your articles sooner or later. The observant freelance mentally logs away any anecdote or incident which could come in useful later.

Relationship features, for example. Do we touch enough? Could your husband manage without you? Would you have an affair? A whole range of emotionally charged subjects which could not be easier to research. Think back to all those snippets you stored away during conversations with friends. Perhaps you can even ask outright. Then simply weave them together – with the help of Chapter 8 – into an article which represents a broad span of female opinion.

Of course you do have to respect people's privacy. Never use anything sensitive without your friends' permission. You can even change the names and circumstances if they do not want to risk recognition. But usually people are happy to help and actually enjoy the chance to air an emotional subject.

As well as helping with relationship features, friends can also be invaluable by sharing other opinions and expertise. Take childcare and parentcraft, for instance. How do parents enforce discipline? How can you prepare your child for nursery school? What do you do when a toddler will not eat? All the answers can be pooled, analysed and turned into practical advice for the women's press.

Whatever your interest, you will find friends who are happy to help. Hints on a particular aspect of model making. Advice on looking after an unusual pet. Practical tips for DIY. Ways to save money in the home. The possibilities are endless. Just stop and think about all the people you know and the interests they have. Then think how you can turn their expertise into a saleable piece.

Then of course there are their jobs. Tame experts on tap. You are writing an article about crime prevention for the elderly – know anyone who is a policeman? A feature on basic car maintenance for women, perhaps – got a friend who is a mechanic? And what about choosing a package holiday – have any contacts in the travel business?

Research does not just mean sitting down with a stack of books. It means getting out and about, using a variety of methods to track down the information you require. It can be frustrating. It can be tremendous fun. But for the article writer, it is essential. So know how to do it and then go out and do it well.

5
PEN TO PAPER

MAN AND MACHINE

You have researched your idea, you know what publication you are aiming at and now the moment of truth has actually arrived. Pen to paper. But will you in fact be using a pen?

A few years ago, there were just two choices – you wrote longhand in a notebook or worked directly onto a typewriter. Probably a manual portable. If you were really lucky, you might have access to a new technology electronic job – one-line memory with a correcting facility. Then along came the low-budget, high-tech word-processor and with it, the possibility of doing more than twice the work in less than half the time.

Now people who have never even learnt to type can turn out immaculate manuscripts at high speed on a personal computer word-processor (PCWP). It will not make you a better writer, but it will speed up the physical process of transferring thoughts – via the screen – onto paper.

At the touch of a button you can change words, insert new sentences and move whole paragraphs around the page. If you have never seen one in action, ask for a demonstration at your local computer shop. It will certainly give you something to think about. And if the £300-£400 price tag seems a little out of reach, just think how many more articles you can produce in the time – all potentially saleable.

This is not the place for a dissertation on the merits of various word-processors. Go to a reputable computer centre or ask writer friends which models and software packages they can recommend. Features vary but none of the basic models is difficult to master.

Computer jargon can be off-putting until you get attuned to it, but just explain what you need and an experienced salesmen should be able to steer you towards the right model.

All most journalists really need is a word-processor with a spellcheck and wordcount facility.

Then simply take it home, sit down with the manual and get to know your new friend. It will not be long before you are turning out top quality manuscripts and covering letters with a professional printed header.

But whatever advances technology tries to tempt you with, there will always be people who find they cannot work straight onto a screen. Many writers – including several best-selling novelists – feel more comfortable with a blank page than a blank screen.

If that is you, then stick to it. Do your first draft in pencil on a lined pad and transfer it to the typewriter or wordprocessor afterwards. The physical process will take longer, but if you like the feel of a pencil between your fingers and it encourages your creative flow, it is quicker in the longer run than staring blankly at that empty screen.

WORKING FROM HOME

For many writers, working from home is just as daunting as the prospect of writing for money. There are all sorts of questions to be resolved in terms of physical space, time available and that all important self-discipline.

The important thing for any writer is to find what works for you. And that means choosing your equipment carefully, the time of day that you write and even the place. Experiment until you find the combination that suits you best, but stop and make an objective review every so often. It could be that you would work even better if you made some slight adjustment somewhere.

Organisation is one of the keys to successful writing, especially if you have limited time available. Take a realistic look at your weekly timetable. When are you most often able to write? It does not matter if you cannot write every day, so long as you try to write regularly. If you have a young family, for example, see if you can arrange for your partner or a friend to look after the children while you have a few hours writing time every week.

Think about where you can write too. Are you the sort of person who can only work when it is quiet or do you like background noise? Some people cannot concentrate properly if they can hear the television in the next room, yet one successful writer used to do first drafts sitting on a bench in the middle of Euston Station.

Arrange your work area where you know you can settle down comfortably and where the rest of the family will leave you in peace. And be firm. Insist that you are allowed to work uninterrupted by anything but the most dire emergency. It is not always easy, especially if there are children or teenagers in the house, but there is a difference between working to a companiable background noise and constantly having your train of thought broken by persistent youngsters.

A stock of well chosen children's videos works wonders with the younger ones. Sit them down in front of a favourite Walt Disney and you are guaranteed an hour or two's peace in which to work. If you are plagued with parent's guilt, you can easily balance it off with a story or game afterwards.

Not that it is only the younger members of the family who need careful handling. Partners can sometimes be put out if the usual domestic routine is interrupted. A husband who spends his spare time doing woodwork or DIY is unlikely to be thrilled at having to keep the noise down whilst you are writing.

So try giving the family an incentive to support you. A share in that first pay cheque might do the trick, or, if you really feel that is a long way off, a small reward en route. They will all have to provide moral support in a variety of ways and will certainly appreciate the odd tangible thank-you.

Make sure friends also understand that although you are at home, you are actually working. Tell neighbours that you are embarking on a writing career, otherwise they will be constantly coming round to invite you for coffee, invite themselves for coffee, or borrow a jar of your coffee. It is very easy to give in, especially if you are struggling to be creative on an off day, but down tools just once and you throw yourself wide open to all kinds of non-literary temptation.

Self-discipline also means turning a blind eye to the

domestic chores and DIY which constantly nag at the person who works from home. If you have decided to write for two hours, then write for two hours. Ignore the finger marks on the window, the crumbs under the table, and the pile of ironing in the kitchen. Leave the grass to grow for the rest of the morning, let the door squeak for two hours longer, and resist the temptation to pull at that piece of peeling wallpaper. They can wait. Creativity can not.

Of course it is not always possible to sit at your workplace and be creative, so learn to write in your head – in the bath, peeling vegetables, walking the dog. Keep pads and pencils handy in strategic places and always carry one when you are out so you can jot down that brilliant idea or perfect phrase. Transfer them to your ideas book and then refer to them regularly. The overheard conversation or unusual fact which proved merely interesting today, could easily turn into a saleable piece tomorrow.

Remember too that you can improve your writing techniques without even writing a word. Market research, for example, is work-related but does not involve you formally sitting down at your desk. So you can study other people's writing whilst still sitting companionably with the family in the evening, whilst waiting at the dentists, or travelling on the bus. It will not look like work to other people, but it is an integral part of becoming – and staying – a successful writer.

Finally, make the most of working from home. You are in a privileged position and taking the first steps along a path which could end up in a full-time career as a writer – or as full-time as you want to make it, anyway.

Try these few tips to balancing writing and domesticity:

– Try to have a permanent corner in which to work, somewhere that you do not have to set up and then put away every time inspiration strikes. The dining room table is not ideal; a corner of the spare bedroom is.

– A telephone by your workplace is a boon to the busy writer. Not only can you work uninterrupted, but you will have everything to hand if an important call comes through.

If there is no socket nearby, invest in a portable unit which you can take from room to room.

– Do not get flustered if someone phones at an important moment. Calmly explain that it is not convenient at present and say you will call back. After all, how often do you call someone's office only to find they are in the middle of a meeting?

– If you have children in the house, teach them respect for your materials from an early age. No playing with the typewriter and no drawing on your best paper. Do not be ashamed to resort to bribery if all else fails – your career could be at stake.

– Do not forget, from the outset, to record all the expenses you incur in the course of your writing activities. You will be able to offset many of against any income from writing on your tax return. Writers can claim a variety of expenses including postage, stationery, telephone calls and even an allowance for heating and lighting at home.

– Writing is a solitary occupation, however many people you may meet during the course of your research. Find out how other writers work by subscribing to *Writers News* magazine, joining a local writers group, or, if no such group exists, forming one yourself. You will find the moral support invaluable and the company stimulating.

Finally, have faith in your writing abilities. Otherwise how else can you expect friends and family to take you seriously? Keep at it and sooner or later you will have a letter of acceptance – and a cheque – to prove your point.

YOUR PURPOSE AS A WRITER

You know what you are writing about and who you are writing it for, but do you know why you are writing it? If you do not have a clear idea, you certainly will not convey it to your reader.

Some articles may be written as pure entertainment, others to provide information or give an opinion. Some will set out to educate the readers whilst others may want to enlist their support for a particular cause or campaign.

Of course sometimes an article is written for a combination of reasons. You might, for example, decide to educate by using humour. A simple example would be a personal account of the writer's hilarious first attempts at pitching a tent – by entertaining the reader with a 'how not to do it' approach, you are in fact educating them in how to do it. To emphasise the practical nature of the exercise, you could add a step-by-step guide as a sidebar.

Similarly, you might choose to write an opinion piece on animal rights as a way of drumming up support for a campaign against testing cosmetics on animals. Whatever your purpose, the important thing is to have it clear in your own mind before you actually start writing. Know what you want to do and then ask yourself which is the best way of doing it.

MAKING A SYNOPSIS

The important thing when you sit down to write an article – any article – is not just to launch in. It does not matter how experienced a writer you are, you must tackle each new project in the same way, with a framework which writers call a synopsis.

Eager though you may be to put your ideas down on paper, a well thought out synopsis will enable you to arrange them logically and readably. Look on it as a map which guides you – and thus your reader – from the start of your article to the finish.

It need not follow the most direct road. There is no reason why you can not make a detour round the scenic route to include a relevant anecdote or explore a related issue. But it must follow a logical path. No going off at a tangent in the wild hope of picking up the trail later.

First priority is to gather all your notes. You may have

some material on tape and some in notes. You may need to consult a reference book or sort through press cuttings. Wherever your information has come from, make sure you have it all around you before you start.

You will probably find it easier to organise if all the material is in printed form, so transcribe any taped information for easy reference. And if you have access to a photocopier, use it to copy pages from any cumbersome books. Then spread it all out the floor is ideal and see what you have got.

If you have several ideas on one piece of paper, try the jigsaw approach. Cut them up and move them around until they seem to fit together. Then stick or staple them onto a larger piece of paper so that nothing can get lost.

You will need to arrange your information in a logical order, but this does not necessarily mean starting at the beginning. There are many ways to open an article, as we will be seeing later in this chapter, and very few of them have anything to do with chronological order.

So find an arresting opening – one which will entice the reader to read on – and then arrange your ideas so that they flow one into another. You may find that it helps to have a rough idea of the ending, so that you work logically through the body of your article towards a given point.

The following are examples of synopses for a variety of article ideas:

Smile Please, It's Christmas!

This was a 'how to' feature of around 1,000 words which made a full page in a national women's magazine. It tells readers with little or no photographic experience, how to capture their special Christmas moments on film.

INTRODUCTION: Most people own at least one simple camera; ideal opportunity to capture some unique memories.
Do not need to be technical. Follow basic rules.

MAIN BODY: Getting help from your photographic dealer.

Choosing the right film – basic explanation of film speeds. Films for indoor photography.

What to photograph: do not wait till Christmas Day – capture the preparations at home and in the high street.

People pictures: making them natural. Using flash. Looking for angles. Family groups.

Technical tips: watch the background, distance from subjects, getting down to children's level, high vantage points.

Outdoor pictures: fun in the snow, pets outside.

CLOSE: After the holiday. Getting them processed. Cheaper to get two sets of prints than to order reprints. Enlargements as presents. Choosing a festive photo to send as next year's Christmas card.

Action Stations

Another 'how-to' for a general interest women's title which would have been equally at home in a specialist parentcraft publication or maybe a travel magazine. It offers advice for painless family holidays with lots of practical tips for choosing and enjoying a holiday with children. Words, about 1,500.

INTRODUCTION: Holidays take on whole new dimension when you have children, but does not mean they cannot be just as much fun. If children are happy, so are the parents, so it pays to plan ahead.

Examples of holidays writer has taken with two young children.

Advantage of taking several shorter breaks – weeks and weekends.

Tips to pass on:

MAIN BODY: Five headings, each grouping arranged as bullet points (ie one hint after another with no links in between):

– Choosing a resort: journey time, climate, beach suitability etc

- Travelling by air: flight times, facilities for babies, keeping children amused, amount of hand luggage.
- Hitting the road: passing the journey, games, toys, story tapes, coping with travel sickness, food before and during, sunshields.
- Self-catering: distance from amenities, what to take, what you can buy abroad, where to play, booking cots, high chairs and car seats.
- Hotels: size of family room, baby listening or babysitting, children's teas, kiddy reps.

CLOSE: At home or abroad, do not forget basic first aid kit... Then just relax and enjoy it – you will, if you have planned ahead.

A Step Back In Time

This was a personal experience piece of around 1,500 words for an equestrian magazine about a weekend spent learning to drive two heavy horses at one of Britain's stately homes. A spin-off piece sold to the local county magazine and it is the kind of subject which pops up from time to time in heritage type magazines, travel publications and even the Sunday supplements.

INTRODUCTION: Arrival at estate. Years of riding experience but about to have first taste of driving. Only not behind a nice, small pony. Instead, step back in time and sample agricultural life of 50 years ago...

MAIN BODY: Description of Victorian stable block and its occupants.
Brief history of the Suffolk Punch – now a rare breed.
Outline of driving course. Instructor and his background.
My fellow students – different walks of life. Not all riders.
Grooming. Huge bulk of horses.
Tacking up. Size of animal, weight of harness. Safety tips.
Hitch one horse to a sledge and set off for park.
Early lessons. Progress from sledge to one horse in a cart,

then two horses with sledge and finally two in wagon. Give rides to visitors across park. Amusing comments.

CLOSE: Instructor's final verdict on performance.

Silent Night

This was a humorous piece of just over 1,000 words for a national women's magazine about a nursery school nativity play. The sort of situation which is familiar to all parents – and probably grandparents too – and therefore could find a home with a wide variety of publications.

INTRODUCTION: Son comes home in September excited at prospect of being in nativity play... What is a nativity play anyway, Mum?

MAIN BODY: Excitement turns to embarrassment when required to speak.
Recast in non-speaking role.
Could I provide a costume by end of week? I can't sew!
Eventually got away with dressing gown and tea towel for head.
Following year, at Big School, I dread costume request, but OK – carol concert in uniform.
Countdown to concert. Practises carols in car – misunderstood words.
Pray he will not go down with flu on the day. He does not but I do.
Feel dreadful but go along. Hilarious near-fight on stage.

CLOSE: This year it is carols again, thank goodness, but highlight will be performance he is currently rehearsing in his bedroom with little sister. Amusing wording on poster...

True Love Ways

This is what the women's press call an emotional or relationship feature. There is more to marriage than just good friends, so what makes the ideal recipe? The same subject could be recycled indefinitely using different examples to fit the readership of a specific magazine. A longer piece this – around 2,000 words.

INTRODUCTION: Some people believe you should marry your best friend; others argue in favour of a relationship that is fiery rather than friendly. So what gives staying power?

MAIN BODY: Simple on the surface, friendship essential, but is it really that straightforward? Facets of relationships.
Ingredients for a marriage. Analogy of baking a cake.
Basic ingredients plus variations to taste.
Importance – or not – of physical side. Changes of feelings, passion invariably cools as marriage settles down.
    Case history of being in love with Love, unsuitable match.
    Does not work long term, need friendship and respect.
So need similar ideals and at least some similar ambitions.
Friendship can last a lifetime. Passion more transitory.
    Case history of girl who falls for colleague at work.
Passion for someone else is big threat to a marriage but what about passion of a difference sort – partners who argue. Reconciliation fun but interruptions from children...
    Amusing anecdote.

CLOSE: Keeping marriage alive, physically and emotionally. Few tips. Comfort of being able to relax and be yourself with spouse.
    But do not get too comfortable – you might both enjoy an unexpected slice of passion cake...

The Charmer

This was a 1,500-word interview for a woman's magazine with tv and film actor Nigel Havers. Hung on the topicality peg of a new television drama series, it looked back over his major roles as well as probing his private life and guessing what makes him tick.

INTRODUCTION: New series. Very different role. Why taking such a controversial part?

MAIN BODY: Background to series, first production from his own company. Where idea came from. Research into character. Choice of other actors. Where filmed.
Has filmed all over world. Anecdotes from foreign travels to uncomfortable locations.
Uncomfortable situations closer to home – physical injury incurred during one star part. That role set him up as Mr Nice Guy.
His background. Family, acting career, early roles, big break.
Always busy. Away from the camera... family, hobbies, interests.
Future. Plan his career?

CLOSE: Like to be remembered for any particular achievement?
Surprising reply...

Room With A View

This article on conservatories was commissioned by a glossy homes magazine. Aimed at the prospective purchaser, it had to include advice on choosing a glass extension, together with information on new products and innovations on the marketplace. Product details and suppliers were worked into the text as appropriate. Word limit, 1,800, excluding information box.

INTRODUCTION: Once just for the wealthy to keep their exotic plants.
Now a different role. Extension to family living space, often costing less than conventional brick extension.

MAIN BODY: Range of uses from living rooms to kitchens, playrooms to offices.
Deciding what you want. Location, size, access.
Materials. Wood or UPVC. Glass or polycarbonate roof.

Double glazing. Air gap. Type of glass. Additional heating
 needed?
Security. Locking systems.
Choosing a company. Supply and fit or supply only?
 Planning
permission.
The cost. As much as you want, but... Designs.

CLOSE: Once built, flooring, blinds and furnishings...

INFORMATION BOX: List of suppliers with names,
addresses and telephone numbers.

These are just a few examples of successful synopses. The
same framework will hold good for any non-fiction that you
write, from local history to hobby features, animal articles to
gardening advice. But it is just a framework.

Give the same framework to a group of experienced
writers and they would all write it up differently. The way
they write it up is called style and that is something highly
personal. You cannot tell from reading the synopsis for Silent
Night, for example, how the humour would come across.
Nor the way in which the writer would tackle a personal
experience piece such as Step Back in Time.

But once you have drawn up your synopsis, you have
something solid to work from. You can arrange your raw
material in the designated order and actually begin writing
without worrying about wandering from the point.

BEGINNINGS AND ENDINGS

Not every writer starts working on an article at the beginning. Some work out the body of the text first, whilst others
tackle the final paragraph and work backwards.

Equally common are the writers who cannot write
anything until they have worked out the opening to an
article. Sometimes it comes in a flash of literary inspiration;
some days they can mull it over for hours. But until they have
crafted those few opening lines, they are quite incapable of

organising the rest of their thoughts.

Whichever way you work, sooner or later you will have to tackle the beginning and it has to be good if you are hoping to sell. To quote the editor of one national hobby magazine:

'I always imagine I've picked up the article in a doctor's waiting room and have only a short time to read. If the first couple of paragraphs of a piece do not grab me, I'm going to turn the page and see if there is something more interesting on the next one.'

So an interesting opening is vital if you are going to grab the editor's – and ultimately the reader's – attention. In fact an experienced editor can tell within a few lines whether a manuscript shows any promise, so do not spoil your chances by being sloppy with the opening.

Writing good openings is a skill, but one that can easily be self-taught. The aim is two-fold – a few lines which will give the reader some idea of what the piece is about and which will also tempt him to read on. By now you should have some idea of the type of magazines you are aiming at, so sit down with a pile of back copies and study the openings. There are many different ways of beginning an article and not all of them will be appropriate to every market, but here are a few ideas.

Some articles simply tell you what the piece will be about:

'If you're lucky enough to receive a greetings card from Gwyneth Radcliffe, you certainly won't find a duplicate in your local newsagent. For Gwyneth makes her own exquisite three-dimensional cards and no two are ever the same.'

A straightforward introduction to an article about an origami expert. Similarly:

'Training has become a buzz word of the Nineties. Whether you're starting work for the first time, returning to paid employment after a career break or simply fancy a change of direction, you will almost certainly need some sort of training.'

This paragraph, followed by a paragraph of arresting statistics about the change in working practices, opened a feature on a television training programme. It developed naturally into a short profile of its celebrity presenter who had practised the very principles explored in the programme when he made a career change.

An opening like this can also be useful for a celebrity profile. When you have a high-achieving subject like novelist and politician Jeffrey Archer, it is a useful way of setting the scene:

> 'Jeffrey Archer doesn't waste a minute. He can't afford to. When you're constantly in demand as a bestselling writer, campaigning politician and enthusiastic committee man, you need to squeeze as much out of life as you possibly can.'

A second piece for a different market began:

> 'Ask Jeffrey Archer what he considers to be his greatest achievement and you know he's going to be terribly spoilt for choice. Youngest member of the Greater London Council. Youngest Member of Parliament. Six bestselling novels. Two books of short stories. Two West End plays. Deputy Chairman of the Conservative Party. Which will it be?'

Intrigued? You are meant to be. This is how the feature went on:

> 'So when he suddenly chooses an event which most people have probably forgotten – and some undoubtedly never knew – you realise there's a great deal more to Jeffrey Archer than boyish charm and a millionaire bank balance.
>
> 'Running for my country,' comes the immediate reply. He grins disarmingly at my obvious surprise. 'Yes, honestly. I'm terribly patriotic. I believe in service.'

Of course some articles do not immediately tell you what they are going to be about. Instead they offer the reader an intriguing fact or anecdote and tempt them to read on that way:

> 'Most people invite their friends to a house-warming party, but not Peter and Maggie Taylor. They invited their friends to a house demolition party. Bring a bottle and a hammer! It was, they reckon, one of their very best parties ever.'

This was the lead in to an article for a home interest magazine about a couple who lived in a caravan whilst they demolished their old bungalow and built a Scandinavian timber-frame house. But if you did not guess that one, what do you make of this?

> 'If it hadn't been for the man with the gravy boat, Jill Dyne might never have set up in business. She met him by chance at a friend's dinner party and their conversation haunted Jill so much she knew she just had to do something about it.'

Now who could resist reading a bit further into that one. Incidentally, Jill runs a china matching service. Did you guess?

This opening couples intrigue with what the media call the 'aah' factor. Children and animals all have an 'aah' rating – and not just in the women's press. Pick up any popular newspaper and you are bound to find at least one picture story that falls into this category.

> 'Life is one long round of discovery for an active young dog like Queen. New smells to be sniffed. New games to be played. New objects to be investigated. But there's one thing that's guaranteed to stop Queen dead in her tracks – the sound of a bell ringing.'

Now the feature could have begun something like this:

'Everyone's familiar with Guide Dogs for the Blind, but how many people know about Hearing Dogs for the Deaf?' But it is bland, dull and it fails to exploit the 'aah' factor which so often makes articles sell.

So you can start an article off by revealing what it will be about or you can do the opposite. You can also combine the two by revealing an intriguing side to a given subject. This works particularly well with profiles of well known personalities. Try this one about popular tv botanist Dr David Bellamy:

> 'David Bellamy adores children. In fact he happily admits he'd like 30 of them. So it comes as quite a shock to hear him say he wishes he'd never had Rufus, the eldest of his five children.'

> '"I sometimes wish I'd never brought a child into the world to face the problems he'll have to face," David says frankly. "That's why I've spent a large part of my life trying to solve those problems."'

David also adopted four children of different nationalities – hence his family of five. A slightly offbeat angle to a much-exposed personality. Then there was this very different angle on writer, gardener, and broadcaster Alan Titchmarsh.

> 'Most people's idea of a family room includes comfortable armchairs, a colour television and all the clutter that most families need to relax. Not so tv gardener Alan Titchmarsh and his wife Alison, for when they built an extension on their rural Hampshire home, they had a very different room in mind.'

> 'Affectionately dubbed The Orangery because of its elegant design, the Titchmarsh extension is the perfect place for a family whose collective passion is performing.'

This next one combines animals with intrigue and personality – a real winning combination:

'David Taylor is certainly a man of surprises. Not only is he the only vet in Britain with an actor's Equity card, but he's probably one of the few vets who doesn't actually keep a pet.'

The reason being that David is a zoo vet, whose unique skills are in demand all over the world, keeping him constantly on the move.

Totally different in style is the personal approach, the sort of opening to a personal experience piece such as this family holiday feature:

'I have to admit that I've never been the intrepid sort when it comes to family holidays. Backpacking in Nepal with a toddler has never appealed and even the thought of the Eastern Mediterranean is more than I can handle with a faddy five-year-old. Some people do it, I know, but not me.'

'So this time we decided to try Jersey – and soon wondered why we'd never done so before.'

Not only does this show that the writer has personal knowledge of his or her subject, it also has the added bonus of reader identification. A combination which should tempt a lot of parents into reading the article.

Here is reader identification of a different type:

'If you're one of the millions of women who'll be celebrating the start of the 1990s without a regular man in your life, take heart. Experts claim this is the decade that single women have been waiting for.'

It also incorporates 'expert' information which adds weight and topicality to the feature. A staggering statistic or fascinating fact would work just as well. Quotations can make good openings, but if you are reaching for a dictionary of quotations, do try and pick one that has not already been done to death. Far better if you can get an original quote – a leading authority, for example, or well-known public figure.

Once you get the hang of writing openings, you will find that the possibilities are endless. In fact they are almost an art form on their own. Study other people's at every opportunity and apply their ideas to your own subject matter.

The way you close an article is important too. Nobody is going to turn to the end of a piece before deciding whether to read it or not, but you need to leave the reader feeling satisfied. No editor will want to buy an article that starts with a bang but tails away lamely at the end, any more than a reader will want to persevere with reading it.

The trick then is to keep the momentum and interest going through the middle of a piece and work towards a strong close. You do not have to leave the reader gasping at your originality or wit, but you must leave him feeling that the subject has been thoroughly explored and concluded.

And remember. A good ending can stick in the mind long after the reader has turned the page to the next article. Leave an editor like that and you could find him eager for more of your work.

Unfortunately endings are less easy to analyse than are openings. Taken out of context, endings can lose some – possibly all – of their impact. However they are quite easy to analyse on your own, so take every opportunity to study examples in your target magazines.

Why does this ending work well? Or perhaps it does not. Could it have been improved upon? Could the article have been given an alternative ending? Why do some types of ending work well on certain pieces? Look at the way the close of a piece relates to the beginning and to the rest of the text, and study the different ways there are of drawing to a conclusion.

Before you start writing an article, it helps to have at least a rough idea of how it will end. That way you can be sure that the main body of text follows a logical progression towards your final point. So before you even write a word, look through your notes and see if something sticks out as an ending with impact. A strong quote, for example. A startling statistic or appealing anecdote.

Of course not every type of article lends itself to a dramatic end, but do not despair. There are other ways. You can come round full circle, ending up the piece at the exact point where you began. You can summarise what has gone before, perhaps adding a one-line comment of your own. You can look to the future for a positive, upbeat ending, or you can finish an anecdote which you started earlier on.

So look at what other writers do, not just in your target publications, but in every magazine you can lay your hands on. See what works and then adapt it to suit your subject matter. Aim for a neat, well-crafted ending – however short – and you really can not go wrong.

WRITER'S BLOCK

The more articles you write, the more ideas you will have for other things to write about, but there comes a time in every writer's career when the words simply refuse to come. Maybe you have temporarily run out of ideas. Maybe you have an idea but it just will not seem to come out in words. Or perhaps your creativity is being stifled by personal considerations.

If you have an idea, a synopsis will help collect your thoughts, but if your mind is totally blank, there are ways to prod the grey cells into life again:

a) If you do not already have an idea at the back of your mind, sit down with your ideas book and find one you have not written up yet. It does not matter how little research you have done. Start making a synopsis, including in it pointers for sources of reference. If you like the idea enough, you could end up with a saleable article on your hands; if you do not, you will at least have got back into writing mode.

b) No ideas at all? Then write a letter to a friend you have neglected – we all have them. Tell him or her everything that has happened since you were last in contact. All the news, the chat, the gossip. Words soon start to flow when you are writing about something close to you and you may even throw up an idea for a marketable piece.

c) Think about what has happened to you over the last week. Choose one incident and write it up in letter form. Then reduce it to fit on a postcard. Finally, cut it still further to fit in a telegram. Great for concentrating the mind – and the writing.

d) Write a reader's letter to your favourite magazine – an anecdote perhaps or a response to an article they have already published. Better still, write several letters to a variety of markets. Many experienced writers began with reader's letters and still supplement their income with them once they are established.

e) Write about how you feel today and why – not just about the frustrations of suffering from writer's block, but about home, family, the world in general...

Writing when you do not feel like it can actually be quite hard work, so give yourself an extra incentive by rewarding yourself when you have produced a certain number of words or pages. Quantity not quality for once – you can work on the quality later.

Promise yourself a cup of coffee, a chocolate biscuit, ten minutes reading a magazine, or something else which you know will spur you into putting something down on paper. And remember, it does not matter what you put down, just so long as you write something.

If you are still stuck after all that, give up actual writing for the day and do something writing-related. Research a new market or sit down with a good reference book and look for ideas. Chances are you will turn up something you can write tomorrow – if you find you can wait that long!

6
A MATTER
OF STYLE

WHAT IS STYLE ANYWAY?

By all means learn from writers you admire. Analyse what makes their writing good and use their techniques in your own work. But always aim to be original. Create your own individual style that will make your writing stand out from the crowd.

Give one of the synopses outlined in Chapter 5 to three different writers and you will end up with three different pieces. Even with the same facts at their fingertips, the same basic material with which to work, they will each write an article which is totally unique. That is why magazines never run out of material.

Every writer approaches a subject with his own personal view – and he will write it up in his own individual style. So one writer's approach to an article on, say, country walks for the elderly will be quite different from another's, even if he is given the same brief by an editor. One writer's humour will be very different from another's, just as he will take his own approach to a factual piece.

Of course an expert journalist does not just have one style. He adapts it to suit the market he is writing for, and – it is only fair to point out – he will naturally be bound to a certain degree by the house style of his target magazine. There may only be room for individuality in, for example, the humour or personal experience pieces. All the others may have to conform.

But do not despair. The writer who proves he can write to order is still saying something about his style. He is saying he can be flexible, and flexibility is the key to successful freelancing. By all means let your individuality show through whenever you get the opportunity, but do not pass up the chance of a sale just because you are being asked to write to a formula.

Just as styles of writing differ from one magazine to another, so they can vary within one individual publication. A hobby magazine on restoring classic cars might, for example, carry a humorous account of a beginner's first attempt, alongside a step-by-step guide to repairing the bodywork. In one, the emphasis will be on light entertainment; in the other, on practical DIY. Similarly, a medical feature in a mother and baby magazine will be quite different in tone from the domestic humour pages.

But what exactly determines your style? Basically, it is the words you use and the way you make them work for you so structure, vocabulary and grammar are all important. You need pace to keep the momentum going and, perhaps most difficult of all, you need sparkle to hold your reader's interest. You do not want him turning the page before you have had time to present your trump card.

Clarity

The way you arrange your ideas forms the structure of an article. Like the structure of a building, it needs to be meticulously planned out and made firm before you actually start work, otherwise you will find yourself wandering as you write. So never be tempted to rush straight in without a synopsis, however pressing the deadline.

At every stage you must ask yourself whether you have structured your piece in such a way that your meaning is clear to the reader. An article which is unclear loses credibility and that, in turn, could lose you a sale. So how can you be sure that you achieve maximum clarity? Here are a few tips to help disperse the fog:

– Your ideas must progress logically but not necessarily chronologically. You might, for example, want to open your article with a dramatic incident and then flashback to fill in the background. But do not flash backwards and forwards, leaving the reader in a time warp.

101

So after you have used your anecdotal opening, for example, make it quite clear to the reader when it took place by saying 'All that was four years ago...' or 'In the four years since...'. Never leave him wondering where he is or he will lose interest.

– Remember that the shape of a magazine article differs from that of a news story, which always opens with the hard news. The paragraphs in a newspaper story appear in decreasing order of importance and the item is cut from the bottom up if space is limited.

A magazine article, however, does not follow this inverted triangle structure. Although you obviously want an appealing opening to grab the reader's attention, you do not have to start with the main thrust of the story. As we have already seen, you need a strong opening, a satisfying close and a logical progression of ideas in between.

– Make sure your reader understands early on what the article is about. If it is not immediately apparent from the opening paragraph or two – and it does not have to be – you should explain briefly in the next section of the piece before developing your ideas in the main body of the text.

– Paragraphs must flow into one another, so the reader is led gently but surely through the piece, without even realising it. Never be tempted to drop in a paragraph unless it leads in some way from the one before.

– Refer constantly to your synopsis as you write. If you have done your groundwork thoroughly, you should have no trouble following the prearranged path from beginning to end.

– A common fault with beginners is to overwrite, especially if you have uncovered lots of research material. So be very critical before you start and decide what information to put in and what to leave out. Be selective and ask yourself whether you could not, in fact, write two articles from different angles with the amount of information you have.

– Be relevant. Although it is perfectly acceptable – and often desirable – to include one or more anecdotes in your writing, you should avoid any kind of distraction which might confuse the reader. So ask yourself whether each anecdote, fact, or passage of description really adds anything to your article.

– Never assume that your reader knows anything about your subject, unless you are writing for a specialist or hobby magazine with a well defined audience. Even then you should be careful. A practical DIY title may well be catering for several levels of expertise within the one issue, so make sure you aim at a specific slot.

– If you pose a question or set out to explore an argument, make sure you bring it to some kind of logical conclusion. It is all too easy to get bound up in the dilemma and forget to resolve the issue clearly.

– Remember that a paragraph which spans the screen of your word-processor will be constricted into column widths when it appears in print. So avoid long blocks of text which are not easy on the eye and can be off-putting to the casual reader. Ruthlessly cut every wasted word and make each one really earn its place on the printed page.

– If you are having trouble filling your pages, ask yourself if you actually have enough material to write the piece just now. Although it is fine to flesh out the framework, you do not want to be padding it out with irrelevant material. Some additional research may result in a far more convincing and saleable piece.

Sparkle

What lifts ordinary writing out of the ordinary and keeps the reader spellbound to the end? An elusive quality commonly known as sparkle. Sparkle is what turns a dull read into a riveting one, a mundane subject into an unforgettable one. And – most important – it is what turns submissions into sales.

There are many ways to sprinkle some sparkle into your copy. Try these and you are well on the way:

– Pace is important. You need to maintain both the momentum of your article and your reader's interest. One simple trick is to vary the sentence length. Short, staccato sentences, for example, add drama, especially if recounting an incident. But do not overdo it. Balance them off with longer sentences to slow the pace down slightly. You need to keep the article moving forward, but not always at the same rate.

– Dialogue is a wonderful way of altering the pace and injecting a little human interest. No immediate dialogue to drop in? Then dramatise a situation by writing it up in dialogue. A few lines can make a dramatic difference.

– Drop in a quote, so long as it is relevant, of course. Quotations liven up the most undramatic copy. So if you gleaned some of your information in an interview, pick out some choice quotes. A local history article for a county magazine will be much brighter if you include a few words from the museum curator, the churchwarden, or the chairman of the Town Council, rather than writing up all your information in the third person.

– A line or two of description coupled with a quote, helps bring characters alive in a non-fiction piece. So if you are quoting a young mother about her experiences of workplace crèches, for example, you might write something like this:

'The only disadvantage is having to take the children to work on the train with me,' says Elaine, a marketing executive who spends an hour every day travelling to work with three-year old Thomas and baby Michelle.'

One simple sentence which builds up a picture of Elaine and explains her authority for speaking on the subject.

– Statistics can be dramatic or deadly, depending on how you use them. Some are instantly understandable; others only meaningful if you relate them to something more everyday. So if you are quoting the size of something very large, for instance, relate it to the equivalent number of football pitches or a line of London buses.

– Anecdotes can make or break an article. Used well, they can reinforce the point you are trying to make or the information you want to convey. But do not just string them together and expect people to draw their own conclusions.

I once judged a manuscript about things that children swallow. There were lots of excellent examples, but the author had assumed that the reader would understand what preventive action to take from the case histories given. She therefore had not bothered to point them out. Instead she should have used her anecdotes to illustrate well defined safety measures, backed up by a checklist at the end.

– Human interest sells articles. One of my writing students once submitted a piece on caring for the elderly. Pitfalls, things to be aware of, help available, how it can affect the family, building a granny flat, and so on. Lots of practical information written by a lady who works for the social services and therefore has lots of experience of the problem.

But the article was dull. Although she was writing about a people problem, the article lacked human interest. So I advised her to introduce anecdotes, snatches of dialogues and case histories, using fictitious names and altering any unusual facts to protect her subjects' anonymity. She rewrote it, opening with a story which grabbed the reader, and carried through her argument with lots of lively illustration. Result? Copy which both sparkled and sold.

Grammar And Vocabulary

You do not need a degree in English to write for publication. Or even an A-level. Anyone who can speak and write everyday English should be able to sell to a wide variety of markets. An instinctive feel for the language is often much more important than formal grammatical know-how.

Articles written in a chatty style are the norm in consumer titles nowadays. This is good news for writers, because being natural, it is easy to write. It is also friendlier, which instantly makes for a greater rapport with the reader. You can talk to them directly if you wish by using the pronoun 'you', rather than writing everything in the third person.

Of course there are times when too chatty a style would be inappropriate, but even so, the trend is towards copy that is light and easy to read, even amongst some of the more literary publications.

This light tone means that you are basically writing as you might speak, so the words you choose will be easy to understand. However we do not usually stop to think about what we are saying. We may think about the meaning – before we broach something sensitive, for example – but we do not think about the actual words we are using.

When you are writing, however, you do have time to think about them, to make sure you use the most appropriate words and to check you do not use the same one twice. Remember that words can convey mood as well as meaning, so ask yourself whether the ones you have used have fulfilled their purpose. Could you have found more appropriate ones?

A good book on grammar and syntax, will help you find your way around the English language, but there is a lot to be said for the feel of a piece of writing. Listen to the rhythm when you read it out loud. Just as the pace is dictated by your contrasting sentence lengths, so the mood must be enhanced by the words you employ. Make them work for you, not against.

Here are just a few basic tips which should help you use your vocabulary to its best advantage:

– Learn to write tight and not waste words. Never use two words where one will do. Why say 'They happen to be' for 'They are', 'On several occasions' for 'several times', 'used to be' instead of 'was'? Similarly, in the sentence 'The book was reprinted last year and it has now been filmed for television', you do not need the word 'it'. So take it out.

– Do not use a complicated word just for effect. Simplicity is generally best. You do not want to trip the reader up and interrupt the flow of your piece. You will either have him reaching crossly for the dictionary or find he does not bother and misses your point altogether.

– Do not use clichés – '... till the cows come home', 'pitch black', 'raining cats and dogs' and so on. We all say them, but if you use something so unoriginal in print, the editor will start to wonder what else in your article is unoriginal.

– If you work on a word-processor, do not rely on the spelling checker. Wonderful though they are for spotting spelling errors and counting words, they cannot differentiate between usage and spelling. So it would not, for example, spot the errors in 'The dog came hear' and 'He asked her if she could here'.

– Do not split infinitives. One of the basic rules of English grammar which we do everyday in speech but should never do in print. So, as you will soon find out, 'The only way to get better at writing is actually to sit down and write', not 'The only way to get better at writing is to actually sit down and write'.

– Do not use too many adjectives. We all want to paint a picture with the words we use, but beware of saturating the canvas in paint. Overload your nouns with adjectives and you will end up with copy which is difficult to read and could even be verging on the hilarious.

– Do not try and qualify a noun when no qualifier is necessary. You cannot have a 'baby lamb' any more that you can 'shout loudly' or be 'rather unique'. A lamb is, by definition, a baby sheep; any form of shouting is loud; and a thing is either unique or it is not.

– Watch out for unnecessary adverbs too. They have the same effect as adjectives. Instead look for stronger verbs which signify the meaning you wish to convey. For example, 'He ambled' says more than 'He walked slowly'; 'He edged his way along the cliff face' is more descriptive than 'He moved carefully'.

– Remember that the active voice is stronger than the passive. 'He smashed the vase against the wall' carries more weight than 'The vase was smashed against the wall'. And on the subject of verbs, choose words which convey some kind of positive action rather than the vague 'to be'.

– Never forget that rules are made to be broken. If you are writing chatty copy for a popular magazine, it is quite alright to use 'can't', 'don't', etc. You can even start sentences with 'And' and 'But', provided you do it sparingly. Use your common sense and do your market research thoroughly to make sure you adopt the right style for the publication.

Punctuation

This is not a book on punctuation, but if you know you are not very good at putting your colons and commas in the right place, it is worth brushing up your technique with a good reference book. Alternatively, enlist the help of an expert friend – a tame English teacher who is willing to proofread can be of invaluable help to the novice writer.

A misplaced punctuation mark not only makes your copy difficult to read, it can also change the meaning altogether. Most people can get by with careful use of the comma, full stop and quotation marks, but do learn how to use them properly.

One of the most common mistakes is the placing of the apostrophe in 'It's' and 'Its'. In the first example, the apostrophe replaces a letter – in this case the 'i' of 'is', so this form would be correct for 'It's raining today'. 'Its' is possessive – belonging to – as in 'The flat has its own garage.'

Many people misplace quotations marks when reporting speech. If you have several paragraphs of speech by the same person, one after another, you only close the inverted commas when that person finishes speaking, not after every paragraph.

So:

'I began working from home when my first child was born,' explains Rosemary, who now runs a successful dressmaking business from an upstairs room. 'It seemed the ideal way to combine children and a career.

'Gradually I built up a regular clientele who gave me more and more freedom to design garments for them.'

Rosemary's customers come from a wide area around...

Another punctuation mark to use cautiously is the exclamation mark – think of them as 'scream marks' and you may not be quite so tempted to scatter them over your copy. If the wording is dramatic enough, the incident humorous enough, you rarely need to emphasise it with an exclamation mark.

And finally, do make friends with the dash, a useful little device for inserting an aside mid-sentence or following on with a related idea. It saves confusing the reader with a succession of commas and helps him to get the emphasis of a sentence right.

LENGTH

If you have done your market research properly, you will know what length of article you are aiming at. Stick to it. If your target slot fills one page of the magazine, do not be tempted to write more – it will only be cut to fit. If you write less, your piece may be rejected as unsuitable at the outset.

Never be tempted to think that your idea is so original, your writing so sparkling, that the editor will make an exception. Occasionally a specialist magazine may agree to run an outstanding feature in two parts, but most editors want the whole impact in one issue.

Counting words is not difficult, so there is no excuse for overrunning. Count up a few sample pages of your typescript, so you know the average number of words you get to a page. Then you will know, as you go along, roughly how many words you have written and how many you have still in hand.

When it comes to the final word count, writers who work on word-processors have it all done for them at the touch of a button. If you are working on a typewriter and submitting a full-length feature, it is perfectly all right to estimate by adding up the number of pages and multiplying by the average number of words per page.

If, however, you are aiming at a tighter slot – say, less than 1,000 words – it is worth your while counting every word. If you have spent time and effort making every word earn its keep, you do not want a sub-editor to start pruning paragraphs to squeeze your copy into an allotted space.

OBJECTIVITY

How much of the writer should come through in an article? This depends very much on the type of piece you are writing. A personal experience article – travel, for instance, humour, or something unusual that happened to you – will obviously require a greater degree of author intervention than a factual account or an information article.

If the angle is less personal but still hinges on your own credentials for writing that article, then establish them early on, before taking a step back and letting the subject matter take over.

So if, for example, you are writing an instructive piece about disciplining toddlers, say that you are the mother of three children under five. If you are writing a step-by-step guide to building a model racing car, say that you have been building them for 20 years and won lots of prizes. Then, having established your authority to write the piece, get on and write it.

A straight reporting job generally requires the writer to be objective – unless, of course, you are exposing some dreadful scandal through a piece of investigative journalism. Generally however, you should aim for balance not bias, and let the reader make up his own mind from the information you give him.

An opinion piece, however, is just that. An opinion. Your opinion. You do not have to give the opposite view, though it might strengthen your argument to do so and then take it apart. Watch for magazines which run a reader's opinion page and remember that there is always scope for short opinions amongst the readers' letters.

Most writers of personality profiles keep themselves in the background, though you can often add to a piece with the odd personal comment about a person's manner, appearance or surroundings. There are however occasions when the circumstances of an interview may justify you writing up the experience from a personal viewpoint and we will be looking more closely at this in Chapter 9.

Best advice, as always, is to study your target publication very carefully and then follow their approach. Let the words flow to start with, but once you have got the piece down on paper, be very critical about how much you allow your own personality and opinions to enter the article.

SIDEBARS

Whenever you are writing an article which gives information or advice, ask yourself whether sidebars would help you present that information more clearly.

Sidebars are information boxes which appear at the side of an article or in the middle of the text, and which save the writer interrupting his flow to give practical information. The sort of information which could appear in a sidebar might include prices, addresses, information sources, checklists... even a quiz.

You may also find case histories boxed separately from the main text. For example, that article on caring for elderly relatives used boxed stories to illustrate the various practical issues tackled in the main text. Some magazines particularly like this approach, so adapt your presentation to suit your target publication.

In fact sidebars pop up in all shapes and forms nowadays – another example of the emphasis which so many of today's editors put on the visual appearance of their magazines.

Sidebars can be put into different sized boxes, tinted in contrasting colours, or given attractive borders. They can be balanced out with pictures or slotted in with eye-catching graphics. Look at any article which uses sidebars and then imagine how different it would look – and how much harder it would be to write – if it were presented in the old-fashioned format of block text with the odd photograph. Dull to look at and not very inviting to read.

A sidebar which immediately grabs the reader's attention may often tempt him to look more closely at the main article. So let sidebars work for you. Make sure they are short, tight and informative – do's, don'ts, tips and lists all make excellent sidebar material but keep them concise. They may need to fit into a single column box and if they are not easy to take in, you defeat the object of having them.

Many different types of article lend themselves to sidebars – hobby, how-to, travel, self-help, and so on. You will even find articles which are composed entirely of sidebars or human interest stories linked by a common theme.

A feature on safety in the home, for example, might be made up of two or three case histories of domestic accidents, plus a number of sidebars detailing preventive measures, emergency first aid, and useful organisations for further information. No main text at all.

As an alternative to a sidebar, you may want to use a foot-note. This type of information box is usually employed when there is just a small amount of information to be included – a contact address, for example, or perhaps the venue of an event mentioned in the text.

But do not be surprise if it 'climbs' up the page and ends up as a sidebar higher up. The page designer is simply using it as he might use a photograph to break up the printed page. Editors know that modern readers prefer something that is good to look at, quick to read, and easy to assimilate, and side-bars fit the bill.

TITLES

An arguable subject, this. Many new writers worry about finding an eye-catching title and spend hours wracking their brains for the perfect headline. There are two schools of thought about titles, but in my experience, they are not worth agonising over. They are almost always changed by sub-editors.

Headlines are important. They sell magazines. Placed strategically on the front cover, they will entice the public to part with their money. Consider the appeal of this selection:

Get Slim, Get Fit!
Work or Children: Can we have it All?
It is never too late to have a happy Childhood.
More Splash than Cash – 50 ways to make money.
A five-step Guide for the first-time Novelist.

Today's public are heavily into self-help – everything from keeping their figure to raising their children, saving money to making money. So a snappy headline which promises a powerful read is a winner. It can also be very difficult for the freelance writer to put together.

All magazines have their own style and that includes their titles. You may have a wonderful title, but the magazine may have used it before or it may not fit the space at the top of the page. So if titles are not your thing, do not waste valuable writing time worrying about them.

Instead aim for a good working title, a label which you can type on the cover sheet and at the top of each page to identify your work. If you can think of something snappy and intriguing, by all means use it. It will attract the editor's attention and – you never know your luck – it just might be what he is looking for to head the printed page.

Of course some subjects do lend themselves to attractive titles easier than others. 'Ten Tips for a Perfect Picnic' would be an attractive coverline for a summer issue of a cookery publication or a mainstream women's magazine. Short, inviting and just right for the readership.

But it is not quite so easy to find a snappy headline for an article on Norman Churches of Hertfordshire. And would it actually merit one anyway? The readership of a county magazine might prefer something rather more sedate. So if you cannot think of anything suitable, simply give it a working label and leave the rest to the editor.

If you still feel your work is not complete without a marketable headline, try looking for key phrases in the article which indicate what it is all about. Study the headlines in other magazines and see if you can adapt them to your own subject matter. Or grab the reader's attention with an intriguing question: Do We Touch Enough? Would you have an Affair? Are the British really animal lovers?

Some writers collect headlines. Just as we all should keep an ideas book, so they keep a book of titles collected during market research. Not only can you then use them to help with your own titles, you can use them as a source of ideas for more articles. Pick a title and simply write your own piece.

One word of warning though. If you do come up with a title you think might reach print, be wary of picking it up in your first line. If the sub-editor changes your title, he may have to rewrite your opening paragraph to fit. And we all know how long it takes to write that...

REVISION

Occasionally I am asked to fill a gap in a magazine or produce a topical article at short notice. It is flattering to be asked and I never refuse, but it is not something I enjoy doing. For a start, a writer needs time for things to settle in his head before he plans his angle and approach, but, more importantly, he needs time to revise his work once it is written.

Revision and – where necessary – rewriting can make all the difference between sale and rejection. Even professional writers rarely turn out perfect copy straight away. If I am asked to write 1,500 words for a magazine I know well, I can probably turn out the right length at the first attempt, but I certainly will not have produced an article which is light, tight and sparkling to read.

Take the sentence I have just written, for example. The first attempt read 'I may well be able to turn out the right length...'. On rereading it however, I realised that 'I can probably turn out...' would mean the same and save me three words. Similarly, I then wrote '... would have the same meaning...'

when '... would mean the same...' works just as well and saves another precious word.

Most writers agree that criticising your own work is a hard-earned skill. There is something very personal about parting with words you have just written. If you really cannot bear to do it, you might be better to stick to writing for your own pleasure rather than other people's. Writing for print is an increasingly competitive business and if you are not prepared to prune and polish until you achieve the best possible result, then you are unlikely to make it to the first cheque.

One of the best ways to develop your critical faculties is to criticise other people's work – preferably in the raw. Your market research skills will enable you to analyse published work, but the printed article has already been bought by an editor and polished by a sub-editor. What you need to study is basic raw material.

My best training in the art of literary criticism came when I worked on the staff of a company's in-house newspaper. As well as original feature writing, I often had to work someone else's copy into shape – anything from a managerial report of a departmental project to a match report by the firm's rugby club captain.

I soon learnt that most people waffle when they get a pen in their hand. They include far too much unnecessary detail, they repeat themselves, and they almost always write in chronological order, burying the all-important result at the end of the story.

Not many new writers will be lucky enough to have that sort of training, but there are alternatives. Swap manuscripts with a like-minded friend or, better still, join a writers circle where you will be able to hear readings of other people's work. Learn by other people's mistakes and then apply what you have learnt to your own writing.

When you first start work on a new piece, the important thing is to get something down on paper. Assemble your material, make your synopsis, and sit down to write that first draft. Then leave it, certainly overnight and longer if your deadline will allow. When you come back to the manuscript fresh after a few days, you will find you can be far more objective.

So what should you be looking for?

– Length
Chances are your article will be too long rather than too
short. If so, you may be able to lose some of the excess by
taking out an unnecessary anecdote or block of information.
Can you tighten up some of the sentences, choose shorter
phrases, or substitute single words where first you used two or
more?

If you have the opposite problem and have fallen short of
your target, can you include some more information, expand
an anecdote, or include some evocative description? But ask
yourself whether you really need to do some more research
before your article will really stand up on its own.

– Style
Read your article out loud. Does the opening really make you
want to read on? If not, work on an alternative. Do you
stumble over any of the words or sentences? Have you altered
the pace by varying your sentence length? Have you made the
most of any dramatic incidents or startling statistics?

Think too about the look of the printed page. Today's magazines want short paragraphs that are easy on the eye and
therefore enticing to read. Have you lumped your article
together into great blocks of text which are offputting before
the reader even starts?

Is the style right for your target magazine? Is the language
too formal or too chatty? Make sure the words you choose
are appropriate to your readers and that you build up the
right rapport with them. You do not want to talk down to
them, nor do you want to alienate them by assuming a degree
of knowledge they may not actually have.

Words are evocative. Have you chosen the right ones for
the mood of your piece? Make sure you have not littered your
copy with adjectives and adverbs when you could choose
stronger nouns or verbs. Watch out for clichés, unoriginal
comparisons or examples. Try to be original every time.

It is very important to doublecheck facts, dates and

spellings. A misplaced figure or a misspelt name instantly reflects on your credibility as a writer. At best, the editor spots it and begins to wonder what else might be inaccurate. At worst, a reader spots it and complains to the editor. Result? One market for which you will never write again.

Finally, ask yourself honestly whether the writing really sparkles. Could you brighten it still more by injecting a touch of humour, telling a little story, or simply using more appropriate words? It could make all the difference between acceptance and rejection.

– Aim

Remember why you decided to write the piece. Have you achieved what you set out to do? Check that you have progressed logically and consistently along your prearranged path. Your paragraph transitions should be so smooth that your reader is hardly aware of moving through the article.

Make sure your meaning is clear at all times. You do not want to confuse the reader by going off at a tangent. And what about the ending? Have you left your reader feeling satisfied or will he be disappointed at the final paragraph?

The Moment Of Truth

Some people revise more than others. Some articles need revising more than others. But sooner or later, you will have to accept that you cannot do any more.

Important though it is to have time to reflect on what you have written, there is also a danger that if you leave it too long, you begin to lose all confidence in what you have done. Read it too many times and you not only miss mistakes, you begin to doubt that your work is any good at all.

You will not know unless you send it away, but before you do, there are a few things you ought to know. You can, of course, just consign your manuscript to the letterbox, confident that you have addressed it to the most suitable publication and written it to the best of your ability.

Or you can increase your chances of success still further with a little preliminary marketing. Read on.

7
INTO THE MARKETPLACE

APPROACHING AN EDITOR

There are two very important things to bear in mind before you submit anything to an editor. The first is that editors are busy people. Many of them in today's economic climate have only a very small support staff, so anything you can do to make their job easier will only improve your chances of acceptance. This includes presenting your manuscript neatly and professionally.

The second is that in spite of magazine cutbacks, most editors are always hoping to find new writers who can provide them with reliable copy on a regular basis. So the way you market yourself is important too. Very few editors – however well-stocked their filing cabinets – will turn down the opportunity to use work by someone with fresh ideas and a sparkling style.

You can approach an editor in a variety of ways – with a completed manuscript or an outline idea, with a letter or even by the telephone. There is a time and a place for all of them.

Not so long ago, editors were looked on in awe by the writers they graced with acceptance. This, thank goodness, is dying out. Editors are people too and many of them have also been struggling journalists. They know what it is like to be out there and hungry for sales.

But although you will find them sympathetic to the jobbing journalist's lot, never waste their time – or yours – by submitting sloppy material. Even small circulation, specialist magazines have their own editorial standards to keep up. So make sure you keep up yours too.

Article or Idea?

The only way to get better at writing is actually to sit down and write. So if you are just starting out on your writing career, you should get as much practise as you can by developing different ideas through from the initial idea stage to final, polished copy.

Find out what sort of writing you are most comfortable with by having a go at many different types of articles – humour, personal experience, information, opinion, local history, how to, hobby, and so on. Aim at a variety of markets and try your luck with several different editors. Sooner or later, you will find one who likes what you are doing and asks for more.

All writers – even professionals – need practise to keep their skills sharp. They also need to develop those skills to the full if they are to tackle new markets and achieve more sales. But researching and writing can be extremely time-consuming, which is why experienced writers take a logical shortcut. Instead of submitting an article to an editor, they submit an idea.

The theory is simple. You approach an editor with an idea. If he likes it, you write it to suit his publication. If he is not keen, you try another editor. As a result, you save wasting your time on preparing an article nobody wants and the editor saves wasting his time on reading an unsolicited – and probably unwanted – manuscript.

In practice, however, it is not quite so straightforward. Nobody commissions an unknown writer and this does not just apply to novices. A working journalist may be very well known to a number of editors, but completely unknown to the rest. She may have a string of credits to her name, but a new editor will not know if she can write the sort of articles he wants until he sees her copy.

The best she can hope for is that the editor will be sufficiently intrigued by her outline idea to want to see the complete manuscript. It is not a firm commission, but it does mean she is in with a fighting chance. If she has done her market research properly and can write to the magazine's style, she is well on the way to a sale.

She knows that the idea has not been covered recently, that it is not yet in the pipeline, but that it is right for the title's readership. She may even get some kind of brief. The editor may want a slightly different angle from the one she has suggested or he may want to use it to fill a particular slot in the magazine.

Certainly, most editors I speak to during the course of researching Market Index for *Writers News*, say they would rather see an idea than a completed manuscript. A hobby title may receive ten or fifteen unsolicited articles a week; a mainstream women's title may get a hundred. That all adds up to a lot of time for a busy editorial office on a tight production schedule.

But there are still those who prefer to see a completed manuscript from an unknown writer. They argue, quite rightly, that they would need to see the final copy anyway before they make a decision, so the writer might as well send the manuscript in the first place.

As a writer you cannot possibly know which approach is preferred. If in doubt, try phoning the editor's secretary or a member of the editorial team. Simply say that you are a freelance writer who has an idea you think would suit the magazine and ask whether they would prefer to receive an outline idea or the finished manuscript.

Many new writers worry that an editor will steal an idea from an unknown writer and give it to one of his regular contributors to develop. The risk however is minimal. Editors are an ethical bunch and therefore highly unlikely to resort to anything so underhand. Anyway, they might just discover a sparkling new talent by allowing a new contributor to work up his own idea, and no editor can afford to miss that possibility.

Letter or phone?

The phone is a useful tool for establishing the best way of approaching an editor, but how useful is it when it comes to actually submitting an idea? Should you send your idea in a query letter or present it over the phone?

The big advantage with the phone is that it is immediate. You do not have to wait for a letter to be read and answered. The disadvantage is that you have no way of knowing when to time your call. You might catch the editor in a quiet moment over coffee, but you could just as easily call in the middle of a production crisis.

The result may be immediate, but it may not be the one you want. A busy editor will probably just tell you to write in. If he is really busy and in a bad mood, he will just simply say no. Not quite the productive discussion you wanted.

So until you have established yourself as a regular contributor to a magazine, you are probably safer to submit your outline idea by letter rather than phone. It is certainly far less nerve-wracking and can always be followed up by a phone call later if the response is slow.

If you have not had a reply within two weeks, you are perfectly justified in making a telephone enquiry. Just politely ask whether the editor has had time to consider your ideas, as you would like to offer them elsewhere if he is not interested.

However there are times when a phone call is the only way to get the response you need. If you suddenly have the opportunity to write a topical article, you will need to determine your market and work to a given deadline.

In this instance, you have no choice but to phone, but before you do, make sure you are well prepared. The success of your proposed article could well rest on your telephone sales technique:

– Ring the switchboard to find out the name of the editor or features editor. It may be listed in the small print of your target magazine, but staff do change, so make sure you have the most up to date information in front of you. It is so much more personal – and professional – to address an editor by name rather than by job title.

– Think your idea out carefully so you can present it clearly and concisely. Make sure you emphasise the key points, including any topicality tie-in such as an anniversary or the publication date of a new book.

– Make sure you know the magazine you are aiming at. If your article will fit neatly into a particular section of the magazine, place it quite clearly in the editor's mind.

– Have a pen and paper ready to jot down any brief that the editor might give you. In fact it is a good idea to make a checklist of points to ask before you even pick up the phone – angle, length, deadline, photos, and so on. And do not put the phone down till you have asked each one. You might also wish to ask what fee you can expect – subject, of course, to the editor liking the final copy.

– Arrange yourself comfortably by the phone, preferably with your paper on a flat surface rather than balanced on your knee. Make sure the washing machine is not about to go into top spin and that the cat will not be miaowing to go out, then take a deep breath and dial.

– If the editor is out, ask when it is convenient to call back. If you leave a message, you leave yourself at his mercy and may have an agonising wait for a reply. After all, why should he call a writer he does not even know? So say that you will call back – at his convenience, of course.

– When you do get through, speak slowly and clearly. First impressions count and an editor is not going to be too impressed by a writer who can not put his ideas across verbally. Offer an idea and you are marketing a specific product, but you are also marketing yourself and your ability to produce that product. Make sure you do it well.

MARKETING TECHNIQUES

Drafting the Query Letter

One of the best marketing tools at your disposal is the query letter, which outlines an article you propose to write for a particular magazine. The aim is to arouse the editor's interest before you actually start work, so take as much care drafting your query letter as you would over your complete manuscript. The chance of a sale could depend on it.

First ground rule, as with a telephone enquiry, is to find the name of the editor or features editor. It may sound obvious, but far too many people still address their letters to The Editor. That is like sending a circular letter to The Occupier – impersonal and, in this case, very impolite. So be sure to get your facts right before you start.

If the name you want does not appear in the list of credits in the magazine, telephone the switchboard for the information you want. And if the name is unusual or could have more than one spelling, ask for the correct one. It all helps to make a good impression.

Keep your letter short and to the point. Give a brief outline of your idea, quoting the opening paragraph in full to give the editor an idea of your style and approach. This may form part of the body of the letter or be typed on a separate sheet, but whichever you choose, aim to be both clear and concise. A rambling query letter is not a good advertisement for your skills as an article writer.

If your idea is a topical one, explain when the article should appear in print, and when you could have the manuscript ready. Magazine leadtimes vary enormously, so make sure you allow plenty of time to meet copy deadlines. More about topicality in a moment.

Give details of illustrations that may be available, either from yourself or from other sources, but do not submit photographs at this stage. Photos should always be sent registered post and this is an unnecessary expense if the editor is not interested in your proposal. But if you have very clear prints available, you may be able to include photocopies with your query letter.

You should also include brief details of any relevant qualifications or background you may have for writing the article. So if, for instance, you are proposing an article on nursery education and have worked as a nursery schoolteacher for the last ten years, say so.

This outline idea is often referred to as a synopsis, but it is a very different synopsis from the one you follow to complete your article. The editor wants a few paragraphs which indicate the proposed treatment and approach, as well as the subject matter of your manuscript. You need a more solid framework to help you with the mechanics of writing.

The editor may also like to know a little bit about you, so a short biographical paragraph will not go amiss. Alternatively, you might like to enclose a short curriculum vitae (cv) giving brief details of your writing career and experience.

If you are already an established writer, list the major magazines which have published your work. This will not sell your idea, but it will establish you as a professional who can – in theory – be relied upon to produced the goods.

If you are a novice writer, you obviously cannot list your sales, but you could mention that you are following a particular writing course or belong to your local writers circle. If not, simply say that you are a regular reader of the magazine and have an idea which you think will appeal to the readership. But whatever you do, please do not grovel.

Do not say how wonderful the magazine is, how perfectly it caters for its readers or any other platitudes which irritate rather than impress a busy editor. He will know you are familiar with the magazine – or not, as the case may be – simply by reading your idea. Finally, do not forget the stamped addressed envelope. If you do, the editor is under no obligation to reply at all.

If you have not written for this particular title before, it never does any harm to enclose a few relevant cuttings if you have them. This means work you have published on the same subject or in a similar magazine, which will give the editor an idea of your capabilities as a writer, and possibly also of the subject matter. Try to keep them of manageable size. A newspaper cutting which unfolds like a roadmap will not instantly endear you to the editor with a cluttered desk.

If he thinks your idea sounds promising, an editor will probably ask you to write in on spec. This is not a firm commission. It means he will only buy the article if the finished manuscript lives up to expectations, but it is an excellent start.

Manuscript Presentation

Once you have completed the final alterations to your draft article, you will need to prepare a final copy for submission. The way you present your manuscript says a lot about you and your attitude. One look at the typescript will show an editor whether you have a professional approach to your work. It is, of course, the content of your manuscript that will sell it, but you must also take great care in the way you present your copy.

Always use good quality A4 white paper for the final version. Type on one side of the paper only and use double-spacing with wide margins for easy editing – at least an inch on either side. Do not start too near the top of the paper and stop well short of the bottom. An extra line in between paragraphs makes the layout clearer still.

Identify each page with a short working title in the top right hand corner and put 'm/f' – more follows – at the bottom right hand corner, with 'ends' on the final page. Make sure that each page is numbered in case they become separated.

Some editors like pages held together with a paper clip, whilst many writers feel more secure using a staple. Whichever you choose, it is unlikely to affect your chances of acceptance. Once you are established with an editor, you can ask which method he prefers.

If you work on a word-processor, your manuscript layout is achieved at the touch of a button. Simply set up your template and you can work to a standard format every time. You can justify margins, number pages and generally turn out a highly professional manuscript with the minimum effort.

A typewriter requires a little more care but will still turn out a professional document, provided you use a clean ribbon and take care when making corrections. An electronic machine with a self-correcting facility is a boon to the inaccurate typist, but do read through each page before you take it out of the machine. Nothing looks worse than a misaligned correction.

If you have a manual machine, use correcting fluid rather than a rubber. Make a hole in the paper and you are faced with retyping the entire page. But never – ever – submit a handwritten manuscript. It instantly singles you out as an amateur. If you cannot type yourself, employ the services of somebody who can. Local papers and newsagents often carry advertisements from home typists and the cost of typing a 1,500-word manuscript is small compared to the fees you could earn from its sale.

No manuscript should be sent without a cover sheet. Centre the title in the middle of the sheet, making sure it is the same one that appears at the top right-hand corner of each page. If you want to add a strapline – a few words of further explanation – centre that underneath.

In the bottom right-hand corner, put your name, address, and telephone number. On the left-hand side, put the number of words, the date and any other useful information, such as the slot in the magazine your article is aimed at and whether or not pictures are enclosed.

If you are submitting pictures, make sure each one is clearly captioned and carries your own name and address. If you are sending prints, type the information on a piece of paper and sellotape to the back of each print. Alternatively, you can number the back of each print and cross reference to a caption sheet. But always use a pencil rather than a biro and never press hard – it will come through to the other side and spoil the picture.

Slides can be numbered with a small sticker and submitted with a caption sheet, but make sure your name and address appear on the slide mount. Self-adhesive address labels are ideal for this – the sort you see advertised in the classified columns for a few pounds per thousand.

Finally, a short covering letter completes the package, the emphasis being on short. If you are submitting an article following a positive reply to a query letter or phone call, simply refer to the initial contact. If this is a cold submission, include the biographical paragraph, topicality details, and information on illustrations.

Topicality

Magazine editors live in a time warp. When the sun is beating down outside the office windows, they are immersed in Christmas. When the snow is thick on the ground, they are thinking about long, hot summer days. As a writer, you need to tune in to their time scale and learn to think six months ahead.

That may sound like a long time, but a monthly magazine may well work three months ahead. Many of them – especially glossies and the hobby titles – establish a theme for each issue, which helps pull in advertisers. This is done at least a year in advance, which means that if you submit an article on a theme which has been and gone, you may stand little chance of placing it. A quick phone call to the editorial office should establish whether your target publication follows this pattern and should also secure you a copy of that important list.

Even a weekly title will plan its issues six or eight weeks in advance. So if, for example, the late July issues go into production in early June, your article needs to be on the editor's desk in April or May. Add on to that the time it takes to develop your initial idea, carry out research, take photographs and generally work your article through to submission stage, and you are talking about a six-month cycle – at least.

Certain issues are bound to be busier than others, Christmas being the prime example. Although many titles are able to attract more advertisers at this time of year and therefore increase their number of editorial pages, competition for the festive issues is strong.

A monthly magazine which puts its Christmas issue to bed in September – as they say in the trade – will be selecting its seasonal features during the summer. If you do not have a firm commission, you should aim to get that query letter or completed manuscript on the editor's desk by May or June.

127

Similarly, many magazines run holiday features in their January issues to brighten the bleak winter months. Again, competition is intense, so if you are hoping to sell a location report or a personal account of an offbeat holiday, make sure you make your approach by July or August.

Just as topicality is important for seasonal articles, so it is vital for those which involve an anniversary, the publication of a book, or the broadcast of a television or radio programme. No editor will publish this type of article once the event has taken place.

A good book of dates will provide the article writer with a wealth of ideas for anniversary articles. But do not just look at the obvious ones – 10, 50 and 100 years past. Try some of the in-betweens or go back even further and see what happened in centuries gone by.

Not every event will be of widespread interest today, but sooner or later you are bound to come across one that sparks the imagination and – quite possibly – the interest of editors in several different fields. But you may not be the only one with the same idea, so you must make your initial approach early.

Recording your Submissions

If you are serious about selling your work, you should always aim to have more than one article out at a time. Not only does this increase your chances of success, it also means that when one manuscript comes thudding ominously back on to the doormat, there is always hope that another will make the grade.

Some editors will reply quickly. Others may take several weeks. It is therefore important that you keep a strict record of where and when you have submitted each manuscript. If it comes back, you will want to restyle it and try another publication. If it is accepted, you need to keep track of when and how much you are paid for it.

If you are only aiming at one or two markets, you may think you will be able to remember all your submission details. You will not. So right from the beginning, devise a system of logging the work you send out, so you have all the relevant details to hand.

Some writers use a card index system. Others prefer a ring binder or exercise book. Whichever you choose, you must get in the habit of recording each manuscript before you seal it in an envelope. Give each manuscript a new card or page, noting the length of the piece and details of any photographs which accompanied the submission. Then make columns underneath to record where you have sent the article, when and the result.

The result could be spread across four columns – Rejection, Acceptance, Payment and Amount – making sure you record the date in each one. A further column could be left for general information such as whether a rejected article was rewritten before being submitted elsewhere. You could also note any comments which may come back from an editor – good or bad.

Keep a hard copy of every article you send out, just in case it should go astray. Articles can get lost in the post or mislaid at their destination, so always make sure you have a back-up. If you work on a word-processor, you may also like to keep all your manuscripts on electronic disc. You never know when you may want to reprint an extra copy or rewrite an article for a new market. Index each disc so that you can easily locate individual articles.

Review your submissions book at regular intervals. It is easy to forget an article which has been out for a few weeks. Editorial offices are busy places, but if you have not heard within six weeks – earlier if the idea is a topical one – you are perfectly justified in making a polite enquiry by telephone.

If the editor has not yet made a decision, you may be asked whether you wish to have the article returned. Unless you are desperate to try it elsewhere, you would be advised to leave it where it is. Otherwise you simply go through the whole lengthy process with another magazine.

All unsolicited manuscripts – commonly known as the 'slush' pile – are read eventually, but it can take time. Mainstream titles which receive 100 or more submissions a week usually divide the pile amongst several members of staff who read them when they have time. Possibles are then passed to the editor for consideration, which may make the process even longer.

Once you become known to a magazine, your work will probably be put into a different pile and be read more quickly. It may even go straight to the editor. Until that day, all you can do is be patient and concentrate on preparing your next piece.

Rejection Can Be Positive

Very few writers sell everything. An experienced journalist who couples good writing with astute market research and self-marketing, should sell a high percentage of his work, but even he can not guarantee a sale every time.

The magazine which accepted all his ideas last year might be running on a tighter budget this year – a very good reason for trying to diversify. A new magazine may like his on-spec submission, but genuinely have no budget to buy it at present.

When an editor says he is fully stocked, he means just that. Magazines which pay on acceptance periodically find that they have used up their allowance for buying in work and must use their existing stock before they can buy any more. Annoying if they obviously like your material, but a sad fact of freelance life.

Even a promising lead can come to nothing, through no fault of the writer. You may hear that a particular magazine is short of one kind of feature. Your kind of feature. But the news may be a few weeks old by the time it reaches you and by the time your idea or manuscript reaches the editor, he may have found just what he is looking for elsewhere. That is freelancing.

But persevere and you may find yourself at the head of the queue next time round. Watch the pages of *Writers News* for details of new magazines and market requirements and – most important – keep sending out manuscripts. Some may come back, but even the rejections have a positive side.

In an ideal world, editors would tell writers why their

pieces were rejected. Unfortunately, they just do not have the time. So the article you researched so meticulously and crafted so lovingly may well come back with a cold printed rejection slip proclaiming that it is simply 'not suitable'.

But do not lose heart. 'Not suitable' can cover a multitude of things, many of which may not be your fault. The editor may have already commissioned somebody to write something similar. There may be an article coming up in next week's issue. He may just be fully stocked. If this is the case, many editors will write as much on the rejection slip.

Of course, the article may simply be wrong for the magazine. It may be too long, too short or too dull. You may have sent it to the wrong publication or sent it to the right one too late. You can not know what articles a magazine is about to publish, but you should know which ones they have recently published. So never skimp on your market research.

When an article does come back, do not immediately write it off. Write it again. Look at it critically, taking note of any comments which may have accompanied the rejection. See how you can retarget it to another publication. You may have to tighten it up, liven it up or find a new angle, but material is rarely wasted.

It is easy to become blinkered to writing a piece in a particular way for a particular magazine. If you really cannot see how to rejig it, ask a friend to read it for you. He or she may be familiar with a magazine which is crying out for your talents.

If an editor cannot use the article you have submitted this time but generally likes your style, he may take the time to send you a personal letter, explaining why this article has been rejected. Do follow-up any glimmer of interest.

It is rarely worth resubmitting the original article with alterations, unless specifically asked to do so. Instead, submit some fresh ideas for consideration. Show the editor that you are keen to write for his magazine and that you have a professional approach to the job.

The most common complaint from today's editors is that potential contributors fail to study the magazine properly – if at all. New writers simply pluck the name of a suitable title from one of the media directories and put their manuscript in the post. The result is a 3,000 word article submitted to a magazine which never publishes features longer than 1,000; an article about teenagers sent to a title which sells to parents of the under-fives.

If you are aiming at a limited circulation title which is difficult to get hold of through your newsagent, you need only telephone the editorial office to get hold of a copy. Offer to pay, of course, but many editors will send you last month's copy for free. They may also publish a list of contributors' guidelines – or tip sheet – which details the requirements of the magazine.

But if the magazine is readily available on the bookstalls, you have no excuse. Get hold of several copies and dissect them thoroughly before making your approach. This will dramatically reduce your chance of rejection.

Another common – and somewhat surprising – complaint comes from editors who react positively to query letters. Many have asked writers to submit an article outlined in synopsis form, only to find that the finished feature bears no relation to the initial idea. So do stick to the treatment and angle summarised in your original letter if you seriously want to make a sale.

ACCEPTANCE AND AFTERWARDS

Congratulations! The editor has written back and accepted your piece for publication. But there are a few things you should know before you finally accept his offer.

Copyright

Most magazines buy First British Serial Rights (or FBSR), which gives them the right to publish your work once in this country. After that, copyright reverts to you and remains yours or your heir's until 50 years after the end of the calendar year of your death.

In practice, you are unlikely to sell Second BSR. Few editors want something that has already been published in this country. You may, however, be able to sell your work abroad. Many foreign publications, for instance, buy articles on British television stars if a series has been sold abroad. There are also many general interest topics of international interest.

So if your work fits into this kind of category, it makes economic sense to see what other markets you can exploit. You will find details of overseas publications in a number of media directories as well as in the pages of *Writers News*.

A few foreign magazines may have British representatives you can contact, but in most instances, you will need to send your work directly to your target magazine. Remember to enclose sufficient International Reply Coupons for the manuscript to be returned if unsuitable.

Foreign publications do not generally pay large amounts for overseas rights, but find yourself a receptive market and you could generate a nice regular income for very little effort. You might also be surprised at the far-distant magazines which publish your copy.

Back on the home front, be wary of a magazine which wants to buy All Rights. This means that you completely assign your copyright and receive no further payment if your work is published in a sister publication, included in an anthology, or sold overseas.

Very few publishers actually demand All Rights, but it is worth querying them if they do. One national magazine which says that it buys All Rights, admitted that it will agree to First BSR if the writer insists. So insist, even if you risk losing the sale. If your work is that good, you will sell it again anyway.

You do not have to register copyright. As soon as you put something original down on paper, the copyright is automatically yours. There is no copyright on ideas, only on the words in which they are written. So you can use someone else's ideas without permission, so long as you do not use their exact words.

If you do wish to quote somebody else's work, you should not quote more than a line or two without seeking permission from the author or publisher. This can be expensive and is best avoided unless you are sure you can justify the cost.

Fee

What you are paid depends on the circulation of the title and the rate charged to advertisers. The more revenue from advertising, the higher the rates should be to contributors. A county magazine produced with a desktop publishing system will pay its contributors peanuts compared to the big circulation national weeklies, but that does not necessarily mean you should not write for it.

If a low-pay magazine accepts everything you write and genuinely cannot afford to pay more, it is worth considering what you stand to gain in terms of experience and contacts. If, for every three local stories you write, you turn up one which can be rewritten for a national audience, you have a ready source of good solid feature material.

A low-budget publication generally attracts fewer other writers. Many established journalists cut their professional teeth on small circulation magazines, gaining valuable writing experience before moving onto better paid markets. But in these competitive times, it is well worth reviewing some of these titles to supplement your income from other markets, especially if you can write a spin-off piece from another feature with little extra effort.

You can, of course, protest if you feel the fee offered is too low. In practice, it is not advisable until you are firmly established with that particular magazine. Few editors will be keen to take on a new writer who spells trouble.

Far better therefore to make a few sales before you attempt to negotiate. Chances are that once you become a regular, your fee may be increased anyway. A number of publishers operate a sliding scale of rates as an incentive to regular contributors.

At the bottom end of the scale, you might get as little as £10 for a feature in a local or small press magazine. At the top end, it could be several hundred from the glossies and the mass circulation women's titles. Reality is probably somewhere below the middle.

Payment schedule

Just as important as the size of the fee is when it arrives. Best of all are the publishers who pay on acceptance – or shortly afterwards. That way, you have the money in the bank no matter when the article appears.

Many however pay on publication – or the end of the month after, according to their accounting system. This means that if the article does not appear for a year, you can expect to wait fourteen months or more for your money. If it does not appear at all, you are in a precarious position unless you have the proposed fee in writing and can get them to agree to a 'kill fee' – a payment made in lieu of publication.

Be very wary of a magazine which accepts your article 'for possible publication'. This means that they like it, but not necessarily enough to put their money on it straight away. If they keep it and return it many months later, you are not entitled to anything. So if they will not commit themselves in writing now, you may prefer to retract your manuscript and retarget it for a rival title.

You may be asked to submit an invoice to the magazine's accounts department. The format is simple. Address it as you would a letter with your own address and that of the recipient magazine, plus the date. Centre the words 'Fee Note' or 'Invoice' and then underneath put 'To:...' followed by the name of the article, the length, and – if specified – the issue in which it is to be published. On the right hand side, a few lines below, type the agreed figure.

If expenses have been agreed – travel or telephone, for instance – type 'To:...' again and list your expenditure, adding it on to the fee for the article. Send one copy to the accounts department and keep a copy in your own payments file. Once the money has been received, transfer details of the transaction to your ledger and put your copy of the invoice in a payments file.

Getting it in writing

Editors are busy people. You may receive a letter of acceptance for your article but it is equally possible that the first notification you receive is when you suddenly see it in print. From the editor's point of view, it saves him writing time-consuming correspondence, but legally it leaves the contributor out on a rather shaky limb.

Ideally, you should be sent a letter proposing a fee for a named piece of work and stating what rights are to be bought. You then confirm your acceptance – or not – of the magazine's terms and a contract is established.

But even if this happens when you first sell to a magazine, once you become a regular contributor and write to commission, you may well find that you get nothing further in writing. You agree an idea with the editor by phone, submit the piece and wait patiently for your money, without either commission or acceptance being put in writing.

It is a common arrangement which can work perfectly well – until there is a dispute. A new editor takes over, for instance. He has his own ideas about the sort of features he wants and the manuscript you submitted does not fit into them. You may have had the verbal go-ahead from the previous editor but he has gone now and there is nothing in writing to support your claim.

If the new editor likes your style and feels he can use you in future, he may offer you a kill fee as a matter of goodwill. But he is not obliged to. So it is always worth having that commission in writing.

Easiest way round the problem is to write a letter to the editor confirming your acceptance of the verbal commission. Ask him to sign his agreement on the letter and return it to you, in the sae provided.

Non-payment

If money fails to arrive once an article has appeared in print, chase for it. It does no harm starting with the editor, just to make sure he is aware of the situation, but he will probably direct you towards the accounts department.

The cheque is invariably said to be 'waiting for signature', 'on my desk', or 'in the post'. Perhaps it is, but if it is not in your hand within 48 hours, chase again – firmly, this time.

Still no luck? Then a typed statement – same format as the original invoice – and the threat of legal proceedings may be enough to extract your cheque. It may also mean they will not buy from you again, but a magazine which is so casual about paying its contributors is rarely worth writing for anyway.

It may even be going under, so keep pestering for your money before it disappears from the bookstalls and takes you with it. If a magazine does fold, you may be left unpaid for work which has already been published or is awaiting publication.

You may be lucky and recoup your fees once the liquidators move in, but you are more likely to find yourself out of pocket. Unfortunately this is one of the risks of writing for money – indeed of any business venture – and one that you will just have to accept as the downside of freelance life.

KEEPING THE BOOKS

As soon as you start incurring expenditure as a writer, you should start keeping a record of your outgoings. Sooner or later you are going to make a sale and the expenses you have accumulated can be offset against your income for tax purposes.

Small amounts soon add up, so keep a note of all your expenses on postage, stationery, and magazines bought for research purposes. In addition, you can claim a proportion of the cost of capital equipment – typewriters, word-processors and fax machines, for example – as well as an allowance for lighting and heating your work area. The *Writers' & Artists' Yearbook* carries an excellent chapter on income tax and the writer.

A large hard-backed ledger is all you need to record your finances – the front for income, the back for expenditure. Keep receipts for money paid out in one file, grouped together by month, and copy invoices for income received in another. Number each invoice so that it corresponds with your book entry and note details such as title, fee paid, and expenses reimbursed with the date.

Do not think that because you are only earning small amounts, the Inland Revenue will not know about it. They will. At the end of the tax year, some publishers actually send their contributors a notification of earnings declared to the Revenue. So there is no escape. But there is a lot to be gained by keeping careful records.

When you first start writing, you will probably derive your main income from another job. In this case, you simply declare any earnings from writing on your income tax form.

If you decide to make writing your career, you will need to be registered as self-employed under Schedule D and pay Class II National Insurance contributions. At this stage, it is well worth employing the services of a qualified chartered accountant who can advise you on making the most of your allowances and help you to operate your business.

A PROFESSIONAL OPERATION

Set yourself up as a professional and you will begin to feel like one, however small your operation at the beginning. Remember you are marketing yourself as well as the product you hope to sell, so it is well worth taking time to think up a personal marketing campaign.

Start by thinking about the tools of your trade. Are you using good quality paper when you approach an editor? What do your letters and manuscripts say about you as a person? Could you improve your professional image?

Headed notepaper always makes a good impression. If you already work on a word-processor, you can easily design your own template incorporating your address, phone number and perhaps a line or two of job description such as 'Commercial Journalist', 'Travel Writer', or simply 'Freelance Journalist'.

If you work on a typewriter, you might like to consider having some headed notepaper printed, A4 size to match your manuscripts. You can offset the cost against your income tax. Tour the local copy shops for the best deal. After the initial artwork charge, the cost per hundred is not high and fresh supplies can be run off while you wait.

Business cards are also a cost-effective way to boost your image. Two hundred may seem a lot at the outset, but you will be surprised just how quickly they go. Give them to local businessmen and you may end up with a commission for commercial work. Distribute them amongst writers you meet on courses and you widen your network of contacts. You never know who you might meet, so always be sure to carry a few in your purse or wallet.

The artwork for your letterhead or business cards can also be used to make compliments slips. These are ideal for clipping to manuscripts submitted as a follow-up to a query letter. With four to an A4 sheet, they provide a great saving in typing paper.

Prepare a curriculum vitae – cv – which you can keep on file, update and photocopy when necessary. This can then be attached to any query letter you send to a new market. Give a brief resume of your writing career, listing magazines which have bought your work, and any expertise that you have in particular areas, but do keep it brief. The editor does not want to read your entire life story.

Finally, look at where you work. Are you making the most of your writing area? Is your work in progress easily accessible when the phone rings? Can you spread your research material out for easily reference? If not, it might be worth investing some time – and maybe a little money – in reorganising your workplace.

A pinboard behind your desk is perfect for jogging the memory about contacts to chase and payments to follow up. A small filing cabinet provides not only storage space, but also an additional work surface. Even a simple device like a three-tier letter tray can revolutionise an untidy desk and help you organise not only papers, but thoughts as well.

Shop around the budget furniture stores, try your local secondhand dealer, or ask business contacts for any redundant office equipment. A cheap price to pay for a professional operation.

8
WRITING FROM EXPERIENCE

MARKETS AND METHODS

Personal experience pieces are not just a way of starting your writing career. They are an excellent way to keep your career going. New things happen every day and by learning to turn them into saleable material, you have a constant supply of features to develop.

There is a market for personal experience pieces in a wide variety of publications. Some provide food for thought; others offer information or advice. Some give the reader a good laugh; others may bring him near to tears.

A personal experience article can take many forms. Some articles describe something that has happened to the writer – a crisis of some sort, an amusing event, or a holiday, for instance. Others deal with subjects of which the writer has specialised knowledge – some aspect of his hobby, his job, or even his family. The important thing is that the writer has some personal authority to write the piece.

As always, it is vital to do your market research first. Some publications, for example, do not accept first person writing, but might take a 'How to' type of feature based on your experiences. Most magazines like humour, but some accept full-length articles whilst others only take fillers.

Look for magazines which invite reader contributions in return for a specified fee. Some of the mass market women's titles offer generous fees for a strong story which fits a partic-ular slot. On a smaller scale, many general interest and hobby titles ask readers to send in tips and helpful hints.

But why stop at individual tips? See if you can put together a whole article giving tips along a theme. Twenty ways to make money at home. Fifteen fun days out for the family. Ten tips for troublesome teenagers. Look for an opening and then take the initiative.

You may think you are not sufficiently knowledgeable to write for the hobby titles, but this does not mean you cannot write about your hobby for another market. If you are a competent photographer, for example, but not sufficiently creative to qualify for the photographic hobby magazines, try looking for a less informed market.

How about some simple advice on taking good holiday photographs, Christmas pictures, portraits of your child or pet, for a woman's magazine? Start thinking along those lines and the market opportunities are limitless – and perennial. Not only that, you may soon join the 'experts' yourself and find that long-awaited intro to the specialist press.

How much of yourself you put into a personal experience piece largely depends on the subject and the target market. At one end of the scale, you have the piece written in the first person; at the other, a third person piece which simply uses your experience as a firm foundation.

But even a third person piece may give you the opportunity to state your credentials. An article on giving birth can be equally authoritative written by a midwife or by a mother of four. It all depends on the angle. If you think it will help the reader to know who you are, then work it in to the opening paragraphs.

Reader identification is an important factor in successful personal experience pieces. The readers must be able to identify with you, so make sure you know who you are writing for and how to pitch your piece. And of course the wider the appeal, the more likely you are to sell.

An amusing account of one parent's experience of the infant school nativity play sold because, as the editor put it, 'readers all over the country will be going through it with their children in the run up to Christmas'. That is the sort of subject you are looking for.

You will obviously need to obey the rules of your target market in terms of length and general style, but do remember that this is a personal experience piece. If you are writing about a turning point in your life, for instance, or recounting some humorous event, the reader wants to hear it in your own words.

As always, take trouble with your opening and ending. You want to grab the readers from the very first sentence and hold their attention through to the very last full-stop. Keep the pace going and use snatches of dialogue, where appropriate, to inject vitality.

And do be extra specially critical when you come to revise. When you are writing about a subject close to you, it is all too easy to include trivial details which are etched in your mind, but which add nothing to the reader's appreciation of the story.

So avoid the temptation to describe the inside of the ambulance in great detail, the long wait at the hospital, and the conversations you had in the waiting room. If you must include them, be brief. Save your precious words until you get to the heart of the story. Readers are more interested in your feelings and reactions than the colour of the wallpaper.

Finally, always look for multiple angles from your material. If you have a particularly noisy or space-consuming hobby, for instance, you might be able to write a humorous piece for a general interest magazine and an advice type article for your favourite hobby title. Never be content with just one sale.

EMOTIONAL ARTICLES

This is a broad heading which covers articles about personal relationships, crises, or perhaps an opinion piece. The important thing is to look behind every incident for that point of reader identification. Is this a subject of interest to a wide audience? If not, you are unlikely to make a sale.

Take a family crisis, for instance. Your divorce/illness/accident is of no significance to the general public unless there is something in it for them too. A learning point of some sort. It needs to have changed your attitude in some way – perhaps started you off on a campaign or made you reassess your life in a way that may provide inspiration to others.

So what makes your experience stand out from anyone else's? The secret, of course, lies in the way you tell it. The reader wants to experience the crisis with you, to see it from your unique point of view. He wants to know how you felt, the affect it had on your life, and to gain in some way from your experience. So do not just tell the reader what happened. Show him. Let him come inside your head – inside your heart too – and live the experience with you.

But do remember that crises can make depressing reading. Lighten them wherever you can. After all, there can be humour in even the saddest situations. Nobody, for example, could fail to smile at the registration plate of the funeral car which carried the coffin to its final resting place – TCP – a humorous touch that even the deceased would have appreciated.

Remember too that the reader does not need to have had an identical experience. What matters are the emotions that went with your experience. The way you coped with the loss of a partner may help someone else cope with the loss of a parent. The uncertainty you felt about following a new career path may reassure another reader about tackling a challenge of his own.

Writing about a traumatic experience is an excellent form of therapy, but self-help does not always make good reading. If you are not yet able to think clearly about what happened to you, do not try writing for publication. Not until you have come out the other side will you be able to offer anything of value to a complete stranger.

Perhaps you have had an experience which has given you strong opinions on a subject – factory farming, for instance, state education, or even something as ordinary as supermarket queues. If so, try airing your views in print. You may need facts and figures to back up your argument, some relevant anecdotes and perhaps some quotes from leading campaigners or public figures.

Some magazines provide a dedicated opinion forum. One women's magazine, for instance, publishes a one-page soapbox piece every month by a male writer. Some opinion pieces make light reading, some are deadly serious, but all

143

must be original and thought-provoking.

Stick to the point, write tight and – where appropriate – write light. But whatever your style and subject, always leave the reader with something to think about. If the editor finds himself mulling over your argument in the bath that evening, his readers will certainly do so too.

An extension of the personal opinion piece is the 'discussion' feature, where several people share their opinions and experiences. Women's magazines publish a lot of them. Is fear taking over women's lives? Do you love your child more than your partner? Would you take separate holidays? Are your friends good enough for you? They are all subjects of universal interest to women and – as such – can often be sold overseas.

Think of people who have an interest in your chosen subject. A group of friends will often provide more than enough material for your feature. Just ask for their opinions. If you can get two or three together, rather than asking them individually, you will probably end up with a discussion which takes off in all sorts of directions you had not expected. Just what you want!

When you come to write up your material, however, be sparing with your quotes. Tighten them to leave just the essentials and make sure that your anecdotes lead logically on. A line or two about each 'interviewee' will also add more human interest.

Ask everyone if they are happy to use their own name or whether they would prefer a pseudonym. Some topics can lead to emotional outpourings they would rather not own up to. So always offer anonymity.

If necessary, change their name and perhaps the biographical details. Thus your friend Jane who has two small children and works part-time in a supermarket, becomes Mary with three kids and no job – unless of course her job is relevant to the argument.

So next time you hear someone pronounce an opinion on something, stop and think whether you can develop it into an article. Chances are you can – and earn yourself some money into the bargain.

HUMOUR

How often have you read a light-hearted account of someone's experience or lifestyle and thought 'I could have written that'? Perhaps you could, but be warned – writing successful humour is rarely as easy as it looks.

Even if you are the life and soul of the party with your fund of hilarious stories, putting them down on paper is another matter. It is not enough just to relate one amusing incident, unless you are aiming at the Readers' Letters page. You need several anecdotes around a theme before you have the basis of an article which will stand alone.

Humour – like beauty – is in the eye of the beholder. What makes one person smile may leave another totally unmoved. It is your unique perception of a situation which determines whether or not the reader will find it funny. In the words of the old cliché, 'It's the way you tell 'em'. The successful humour writer needs a subject which has broad appeal and the gift of telling it in a light and entertaining manner.

It is not always easy, but it is worth persevering. Humour is all around us, especially if you have an eye – and ear – for the absurd. People are constantly saying and doing amusing things and many of them will involve you. Even a bad day can make amusing copy, given the right treatment.

Just look for that reader identification, the point of contact that makes the reader think 'I know exactly how she feels' or 'My family are just like that'. Get the readers on your side from the beginning and keep them smiling to the end.

The word 'smiling' is important too. Humorous writing is rarely about making people roar with laughter. They may chuckle once or twice in the course of reading your article, but they are hardly likely to roll off the chair. If you are lucky, they will smile as they read. Keep their attention to the end and you will hopefully leave them feeling good – and looking for your name in the credits next time round.

Markets exist almost everywhere – from women's magazines to hobby titles, trade publications to specialist periodicals. There is hardly an editor who would not welcome more humour and hardly a subject which can not be approached with a smile. But do research magazine requirements carefully. They may have a particular length for their light hearted slot.

Keep a humour notebook – just as you keep an ideas book – and collect newspaper cuttings, overheard conversations, and amusing aspects of everyday life which could form part of an article later on.

If you are eavesdropping on an amusing conversation or noting down some hilarious happening, try to jot down as much detail as you possibly can. Who is involved? What do they look like? What are the surroundings? When is this taking place? The details may seem irrelevant at the time, but may well come in useful later.

Wait until you have got several stories along a theme. Teaching in a nursery school. Learning a new hobby. Family relationships. Office politics. Just because you are tackling subjects from a personal experience viewpoint does not mean you cannot include anecdotes from outsiders. 'A friend of mine went...', 'Not like my neighbour who...' enable you to widen the scope of a personal piece with additional material.

Openings are important in any article but particularly if it is humorous. Funnies are generally shorter than features, so you need to grab the reader from that very first paragraph. Take this example from an article entitled 'Is Anybody There?'

'What do you mean, you want an appointment?' my husband demanded incredulously down the telephone. 'I live with you for Heaven's sake! Can't you talk to me when I get home?'

'I only wish I could!' I countered with feeling. Communications have been a little strained recently to say the least.

Aimed at a general women's audience, this article immediately sets up reader identification and scores with universal appeal. Most of the readers, at some time, will have had problems communicating with their partner. The author then strengthens that identification still more with a few details about her domestic situation – career, young family, not enough hours in the day. The reader immediately feels sympathetic and in tune:

> My husband's worn out dealing with adults who behave, he says, like children. I'm worn out dealing with children who think they can behave like adults. We converse briefly over breakfast (standing up), supper (slumped in front of the tv), and occasionally on the landing (half asleep), when one of the children has a bad dream.

> Hometime greetings have deteriorated into the classic 'Had a good day at the office?' and 'Children been good, darling?' – the answer to both questions invariably being 'No'.

By now any reader who has children and/or a partner should be well and truly involved. The trick then is to keep the momentum going with short, snappy stories – all directly relevant – and light, tight writing. Snatches of dialogue help to add pace.

The reader is looking to see what the author did to help the situation. Did she in fact solve it? There could be a learning point here, as well as an entertaining read. The answer comes in the next few paragraphs – tightly written with plenty of human interest.

Husband is anxious to get off phone and back to work... suggests dinner out. Writer books babysitter, turns down another invitation, and anticipates intimate evening together. Arrive at restaurant to find neighbours on next table – goodbye togetherness. Remembers the time, before children, when they used to do their talking on long country walks.

> But it's not easy holding a serious conversation when you're rambling in the wilds with a baby in a back-pack. My husband's forever bobbing up and down to avoid

braining her on low branches, whilst our five-year old is discovering the joys of the countryside first hand.

'Mum, I slipped!' quickly turns a pleasant stroll into an urgent bolt for home and bath when you realise he's fallen in a cow pat – face down.

Recalls the one weekend they spent alone in a hotel before daughter was born. Son staying with grandparents. She and husband too stunned by the silence to talk – until on their way home. Now, with two young children, weekends away unlikely for a while…

At this point, the article is drawing to a close – about one column inch to go. So how is the author going to resolve it? The pace and tone need to be kept up right to the very last word, not to mention that important empathy with the reader:

Still, we have got Saturday afternoon to look forward to. My son's been invited to the zoo and my parents are having the baby. So we're planning to get reacquainted over a pub lunch and catch up with ourselves on a long country walk.

There's only one problem. I've just developed an unglamorous cold and my voice is going. Anybody teach sign language?

End of story – 750 words. If the reader is left thinking 'Just my sort of luck' too, the writer has scored. Even the reader who has no experience of communication breakdown – and there cannot be many – is bound to know how it feels to have her plans thwarted yet again. The editor obviously did. She bought the piece.

An important element in any piece of humorous writing is anecdotal material. Little stories to illustrate a point. By all means accumulate anecdotes around a theme, but do not feel you have to use them all just because they are there. They need to lead logically one from another, taking the reader forward every time. Be selective and only use those which are both strong and relevant, cutting out any unnecessary detail.

When you finally submit your work to an editor, do not take it personally if the article is rejected. Although editors usually welcome light-hearted pieces, a lot of subjects inevitably get recycled and it can be hard to turn out something fresh and original.

Hopefully sooner rather than later, you will find an editor who judges your humour just right for his readers. If so, you may find a ready market for follow-up pieces. But if too many editors turn you down, ask yourself whether writing humour is really for you. Perhaps you are one of those sparkling party-goers who can keep the jokes up all evening but just cannot connect them on paper.

If so, do not give up. Many 'straight' features benefit from carefully placed anecdotes and humorous touches. Stop trying to be funny and let your personal view of life shine through in some of your other work.

HOW-TO

Advice and instructional articles are popular with almost every type of magazine from general women's interest to hobby magazines, business publications to specialist titles. Make Your Marriage Work. Ten Tips for Troublefree Travel. Fundraising made Easy. How to Say No. Whatever we do, we all want to know how to do it better, which is excellent news for the enterprising article writer.

How-to articles divide roughly into two categories – how-to-make/do (instructional type) and how-to-be/achieve (self-help type). Whatever your lifestyle and interests, you are bound to have some sort of experience you can pass on to others.

Start by thinking through all your skills and experiences, then making a list of possible subject areas. Your job; hobbies; family; holidays; pets; health; illness; domestic situation. Then explore the possibilities of each one in detail. Even if you are no good at writing titles, try and think in terms of cover lines – those few words on a magazine cover designed to tempt potential purchasers:

– Job
Ten techniques for successful interviews. Coping with office politics. How to stay fit in an office. Projecting yourself for promotion.

– Hobbies
Discover your family tree. Choosing a riding school/golf club/evening class. Christmas gifts for kids to make. Earn money from writing/cooking/sewing.

– Family
Find your way through the pocket money maze. Help your child to sleep. Prepare your child for Big School. Brighten up your kid's room. Quarrelsome kids – how to keep the peace.

– Holidays
Choosing a holiday cottage. Games to pass a car journey. How to pack the perfect suitcase. Holidays abroad – making your money go further.

– Pets
Top tips for training your dog. Choosing a cattery. Ten things every pet owner should know. Build a rabbit hutch in under an hour.

– Health
Get slim and stay slim. Low fat food for all the family. Essential exercises to keep you fit. Five health checks no woman should go without.

– Illness
Prepare your child for hospital. Coping with serious illness. Could you be a long-term carer? Drug abuse – do you know the signs?

– Domestic situations
Learning to live with step children. Overspending – twenty

tips to better budgeting. Planning a wedding. Party food for under-fives. Working from home.

Once you have made your list, go through it carefully to pick the strongest titles and the subjects you think you are best qualified to write. But do not be put off if you cannot complete the article from your own experience. Supplement your own personal knowledge from information in your cuttings library or seek out a relevant expert or organisation who can fill in the gaps.

Do not always aim at the most obvious markets. Think who else might be interested in your particular specialisation. Take this article, entitled *Make Money from Writing*, which sold to an expatriate magazine:

'The world is full of secret scribblers. People who love to write and do so entirely for their own pleasure. Some know they have a novel in them. Others prefer to write short stories. And some compulsively record their experiences and observations.

For the expatriate, writing is a rewarding hobby. You can spend as much or as little time on it as you want, lose yourself in fiction, or use writing as an incentive to find out more about your location. But did you realise that you can also make money out of it?'

No prizes for guessing who wrote that one! To me, the content of the article – finding ideas, writing them up and marketing them – was second nature. To someone who liked writing but never dreamed they could sell their work, it was a revelation. Perhaps some aspect of your job or hobby could open doors to other people.

Or perhaps you have simply discovered a better/quicker/ cheaper way to decorate your house/manage your time/spray your roses. It may seem everyday to you, but stop and think how novel it might seem to other people.

When it comes to writing up your how-to feature, the style you choose will depend very much on the style of your target market and the type of how-to you intend to write, so market research is – as always – essential. Step-by-step instructions, for example, are appropriate to a feature on how to make or do something. Bullet points or simply straight prose may be more suitable for an article which tells you how to achieve something.

If you are describing how to make a craft item, for instance, you will need only a short introductory paragraph tempting the reader to have a go. Tell him how easy it is; how satisfying to produce; or how beautiful to have around the home. Then show him, step-by-step, how to do it.

This type of how-to requires the writer to be both precise and concise. Precise in his information about materials required, where to get them and what they cost; concise in his instructions about how to make the chosen item. Keep the text simple and as short as possible without leaving any ambiguity in the method.

You will probably require illustrations of some kind – either photographs or line drawings, depending on the publication. If you can take your own photographs, you will usually be paid an extra fee. Some magazines however prefer to take their own. If you are approaching the editor with a query letter first, describe the sort of illustrations you feel would be appropriate, enclosing an example if you have one.

Some how-to features lend themselves to bullet points – individual points or paragraphs designed to stand alone. For example, an article on things to do with young children could be divided into three sections – Fun in the Country, Fun in the Town and Fun Anywhere. Under each section come ten numbered bullet points.

So Fun in the Country begins:

(1) Take bark rubbings from different types of tree. Sellotape a piece of thin white paper on to the trunk of a tree and rub gently but firmly with a wax crayon – the bark pattern will appear like magic.

(2) Choose a colour and then collect as many different

things as you can of the same colour – white stones, feathers, petals, snail shells and so on.

(3) See how many different types of farm machinery you can count on a country walk...

Any how-to feature connected with children stands a good chance of finding a home, either with the mother-and-baby titles or general women's magazines. Parenthood is one of the most daunting jobs of all and probably the one for which we receive the least preparation. Textbooks are fine for basic know-how, but what most mothers want to hear is what real mothers actually do. So if you have children, see what tips you can pass on.

Look for multiple angles too. Why not an article aimed at fathers? Or even grandparents? A how-to piece about making your house safe for the grandchildren, for example, could well find a home with a magazine for the over-50s.

One of the biggest changes in magazine publishing in recent years has been the growth of specialist – or 'niche' – markets. These are often excellent markets for how-to features and well worth studying for those with particular areas of expertise.

A how-to article does not need to be written step-by-step or point-after-point. It can be written up as a straight feature, perhaps supported by an advice panel in the form of a sidebar. An article dealing with some kind of emotional or self-help situation, for example, should first illustrate the problem, explain why it happens and then suggest ways of solving it.

The opening needs to be strong but concise. Let the reader know immediately what the article is to be about and why they ought to read it, as in this health feature for an educational magazine:

'It's not easy telling a six-year old tomboy that his favourite foods are going on strict ration – for life. My son has always been an adventurous eater but he is still partial to a regular fix of chips and chocolate, ice cream and cream cake.

However Andrew suffers from Familial Hyper-
cholesterolaemia or too much fat in the blood. It's a
condition which tends to run in families where there is
a history of early death from heart disease and affects 1
in 500 in the UK.'

The condition will be new to a lot of readers, yet the opening
paragraphs show that many of them could be affected. The
article explains about diagnosis, emphasises the importance
of good eating habits for all children, and shows what steps
parents can take. Lots of simple but practical self-help ideas.
Similarly, this article about helping bereaved friends.
Another strong opening which tempts the reader to read on:

'It happens to all of us sooner or later. The death of a
much-loved partner, friend or relative. But even if the
death isn't unexpected, few of us are prepared for the
feelings of sorrow that overwhelm us.

Bereavement is a time when we need the support and
understanding of both family and friends, but sadly this
help isn't always as forth-coming as we would like it to
be. Not because people don't care, but simply because
they don't know how to help with someone else's grief.'

The author then goes on to illustrate the situation with a
couple of concise anecdotes, before outlining ways that you
can help a friend in that situation. The closing paragraph
ends on an optimistic note:

'Nobody faces death easily, but the worst thing you can
possibly do is pretend that it didn't happen. By talking
to a bereaved friend about the dead person and remembering the good times, you can help him or her to come
to terms with their loss and start looking forward to a
brighter future.'

A sidebar contains information about an organisation of
specialised bereavement counsellors. It could also include a

checklist of one-line reminders. The aim, at the end of 1,000 words, is to give the reader a new perspective on a universal problem, as well as plenty of practical advice on dealing with it.

ANIMALS

Ask any aspiring writer to list the subjects he thinks he could write about and chances are that animals will feature somewhere amongst them. Most people have some sort of personal experience of keeping animals and, because of the role their pet plays in their life, they naturally think it will make interesting copy. Unfortunately, this is rarely the case.

Pets are like children. If you have one, you think yours is better than anyone else's and that other people should therefore be interested. But unless you have some really original or practical information to pass on, you are unlikely to raise more than a polite smile – or perhaps a glazed look as long-term boredom sets in.

Unfortunately people who want to write about animals often fail to appreciate this. Ask the editor of any of Britain's many animal magazines. They are inundated with articles which are overly sentimental, stunningly unoriginal and – it has to be said – excruciatingly dull. Ten Tricks I Taught Tiddles or Riverside Rambles with Rover are unlikely to find a home with a specialist pet title. Or anywhere else for that matter.

So if you are determined to write about animals, you must first – as always – do your market research thoroughly to find out what sort of material these magazines do want. And then work hard on developing ideas which are fresh, original and saleable.

The majority of animal magazines cater for the real enthusiast who breeds or exhibits his chosen animal. Cage birds. Dogs. Cats. Tropical fish. Some are allied to animal organisations such as the Kennel Club or the Budgerigar Society, which automatically indicates an informed readership. Potential contributors therefore need to be extremely knowledgeable.

Animal magazines are a good market for practical features based on the writer's own experiences. So if you have tried breeding some particularly difficult species, feeding a revolutionary new diet, or building a unique type of animal house, see if you can turn it into a how-to type of feature.

Editors are often short of writers who can produce good instructional copy which is both well informed and easy to read. The constant moan is that most of the unsolicited copy they receive is too frivolous or sentimental.

'Anything to do with dogs, but not in a Fido-ish way,' pleaded the editor of one dog publication. 'No soppy stories about moggies, please,' echoed the editor of a cat magazine.

So refrain from writing about how you took in a puppy from the rescue centre, unless you have a really original angle and can pass on some practical information to the reader. Far more saleable would be a profile of the rescue centre itself or a hard-hitting investigation into Britain's unwanted dogs.

Animal lovers want to be entertained but they want to be informed too. Tell them something they did not know, either to make them think or – better still – to spur them into actually doing something.

Seasonal articles are a good example. Tips for taking your dog on holiday. Christmas presents for cat lovers. Beat the freeze for horse owners. Remember to send your manuscript or query letter in many months ahead if you are aiming at a particular issue or time of year. Other people may have the same idea and specialist magazines rarely have a large staff so the reply may be a while in coming.

Look at what is happening in your area. An exhibition or show, for instance. A new pet store. A pet personality. Given enough ideas, you may be able to offer your services as a regional correspondent. Specialist titles with limited resources often welcome writers who can reliably report on events in their area.

Moving away from the smaller furred and feathered varieties, one of the largest specialist sections of the animal press is now the equestrian market. A wide range of titles have become established in recent years covering practical horse care and riding techniques, through well-defined areas of equestrian sport such as eventing, show jumping and polo. There are also a number of publications for younger pony owners.

As with any specialist subject, you must know your stuff, but equestrian articles do not have to be highly technical. Features on riding techniques or stable management may well be written in-house or by commissioned experts. Many titles, however, offer scope for profiles, humour and other horse-related features.

Of course there are also openings for animal articles outside the specialist pet press. A number of general interest magazines – women's titles, in particular – often accept animal features. Magazines which publish regular pet care features usually have their own resident veterinary writer, so look for something which falls outside his brief.

Profiles of animal welfare organisations are always popular, especially if there is an anniversary looming or the launch of some new project. Include lots of human and animal interest in the form of anecdotes from members of staff. Look at changes in the way they run their operation, emerging trends and future plans. Tug at the heart strings and back it up with some appealing photographs – most animal charities have their own photographic library and all are eager for more publicity.

Look out too for personalities of the animal world – both animals and humans. Pets that feature in popular television commercials or series, for instance. Animals who work for a living, such as police horses, guide dogs, and hearing dogs for the deaf. Photographers. Sculptors. Painters. TV naturalists. Animal people are often quite extrovert so keep a look out for interesting characters to interview.

An alternative to the straight interview is the behind-the-scenes feature. The public are often fascinated by the day-to-day lives of people who work with animals – the staff of a dogs home, the vets at the zoo, and so on. Most organisations are happy to help genuine journalists, especially if they have already aroused an editor's interest, and will arrange for you to spend a few hours watching what goes on – so long as you do not get in the way.

Seasonal animal articles sell well to general interest magazines as well as to the specialist press. So if you have overcome problems with pets on bonfire night, worked out a foolproof system for assessing boarding kennels, or compiled a list of hotels that welcome dogs, share it. Sell it this year and then rewrite it for another publication next year.

If you are writing from experience, you will probably have most of the information at your fingertips, but your article may carry more weight if you can include facts and figures from recognised organisations or experts. You may already belong to one or more charities or organisations. If so, make sure you keep copies of any newsletters or magazines they produce, indexing them for easy reference.

Your local library will stock books on animals, as well as biographies of personalities and possibly histories of well-known organisations. They will certainly be able to provide you with addresses and phone numbers for all the animal charities. Then contact their press offices direct to arrange a visit or ask for an information pack.

You will often find that what started out as one article for a target publication will multiply into several pieces, written from different angles to suit other markets. So long as they are sufficiently different and being sold to non-competitive titles, no-one will complain, even if they all appear around the same time.

So if you uncover a significant anniversary or other topicality peg for a particular animal organisation, see how many sales you can make from the material you have collected. The charity will be delighted and so too, will your bank manager.

TRAVEL

It sounds like the ideal way to earn money – writing articles about your holidays – but travel writing is definitely not the soft option so many people imagine.

Many of the names you see cropping up time after time on articles about exotic destinations are members of the Guild of Travel Writers, people who make their living the hard way by living out of suitcases and following a schedule which would reduce most travellers to quivering wrecks.

It is one thing to write a short article about a family holiday once or twice a year; quite another to try and earn your living out of travel writing. Whilst the average holiday-maker might take in one castle or museum to break up his day on the beach, the travel writer may have to visit several. And whilst ordinary tourists can choose to skip lunch in anticipation of dinner, the professional traveller will probably have to eat both.

Then there is the sheer cost of all this moving about. Although the established freelance can often persuade airlines, travel companies and tourist boards to provide free transport or accommodation, a lot of expenses have to be paid for upfront. Few editors are flush with expenses, which means that museum charges, equipment hire and public transport may well have to be deducted from any subsequent fees.

Having said that, if you are bitten by the travel bug and determined to try your hand at travel writing, go for it. There are openings for travel articles in a wide variety of magazines, provided you can turn out something fresh and original.

There are very few specialist travel magazines in this country, most of them falling either into the trade press or business traveller category. The trade press largely want news items; the business press, in-depth features on travel itself more than location reports.

Some travel organisations operate their own magazines, as of course do the airlines and ferry companies. Unfortunately opportunities are generally limited. Some of the publications appear only bi-monthly or quarterly and do not, therefore, use large numbers of articles. The bigger circulation titles often only commission well known 'celebrity' writers.

Best bet by far is the broad category of consumer magazines, in particular those aimed at women or at specific leisure markets such as camping, caravanning, motoring, walking, and sailing. Then there are the articles which are not strictly travel features but which do arise from the writer travelling to another part of the country – an article for a county magazine in another area, for instance, or some aspect of country life.

A lot of the so-called travel articles which appear in today's general consumer magazines are little more than destination reports. A feature on the Costa del Sol, for example, will simply detail the best beaches and historic sites, backed up with details of where to stay, what to eat, and what it costs to go there. One often wonders whether the writer has even been to the country in question.

Perhaps they have, but many such pieces are written not by people who specialise in travel writing, but by members of the magazine's staff who happen to have been in the editor's office when the freebies were handed out. Even in recessionary times, tourist boards and tour companies still offer a surprising number of 'facility' trips – free holidays in return for editorial.

If you are aiming at real travel writing, you need to do more than regurgitate the travel brochures. You have to get to the heart of a place. Understand what makes it the way it is, the sort of people who live there, and the attractions it holds for the discerning visitor.

As a freelance you are most likely to make those initial sales if you can offer something slightly unusual. An offbeat activity holiday you have sampled and enjoyed. A well known destination at an unusual time of year. Or perhaps a very strong angle, such as Paris for the disabled or New York for the under-fives.

Remember, you do not have to go somewhere exotic to write compelling travel copy. In fact, you do not even need to leave your home town. It may be home to you, but it could be a fascinating holiday destination to someone from the other end of Britain.

Alternatively, you may have spent the last five years self-catering in this country or holidaying with a disabled relative. If so, you will be something of an expert by now and are sure to have useful advice to pass on.

Wherever you go, be sure to do your homework before you travel. Borrow guidebooks from your library, contact the local tourist board for maps and leaflets, and consult the reference books to see if there are any famous people or forthcoming anniversaries connected with your destination. The more prepared you are before you go, the more useful material you will gather while you are away.

Do not overlook the possibility of some general travel pieces too. If you are travelling through several European countries, for example, you could take a light-hearted look at Continental breakfasts – each nation has its own culinary start to the day.

Write a piece on surviving airport delays, packing the car for the Continent, or essential holiday first aid. Similarly, you can collect material to work into a compilation article at a later date – top ten stately homes for kids, Britain's best animal attractions, historical museums, and so on.

Once you have chosen a few possible angles, work out a synopsis and see if you can arouse the interest of an editor – or two. Knowing who you are writing for is – as always – a great help in gathering the kind of information you want. It may also help with your travel costs. Many airlines, ferry companies and so on will provide bona fide journalists on assignment with complimentary travel. It is certainly worth writing to the company press office to see.

When you are packing your suitcase – or rucksack – the two most essential items of equipment are a thick, sturdy notebook and a camera you know well.

A travel writer can double his money by providing a complete package of words and pictures. He should certainly have no shortage of picture opportunities so it is well worth perfecting those photographic skills before you travel.

You do not need to be technically brilliant so long as you have a good eye for composition. The simplest shots are often the most effective. Remember to look at a scene from every conceivable angle before you press the shutter release button. A pace or two either way, a higher viewpoint, or a shot from low-down, may give your picture much more impact.

And never be afraid to move in as close as your camera – and subject – will allow. Many a picture has been spoilt because the photographer stood too far away. So always try to fill the frame.

A ballpoint pen on a cord round the neck is a handy tool which ensures that you are never left scrabbling for a pen when inspiration strikes. Also useful is a plastic carrier or two to protect the reams of literature you will inevitably accumulate on your travels.

Try and familiarise yourself with your destination before you start with the aid of a good map. Once you arrive, a tour by sightseeing bus – or, where appropriate, by river cruiser – is an excellent way to get your bearings. Then leave the organised tours to the tourists.

Public transport gives your the chance both to observe the locals and get a feel for the place you are visiting. In fact mix with the locals at every opportunity. Visit the shops they run and the restaurants where they eat, watch their street games and join in their festivals.

Collect local colour at every opportunity. Fill your notebook with quotes and anecdotes, conversations and characters, fascinating facts, historical curiosities, and humorous happenings. Never miss the chance to try out your linguistic skills – or lack of them – on taxi drivers and hotel staff, tourist guides and shopkeepers. Try new foods, identify new flowers, investigate new names. They will all bring your travel writing alive.

Of course travelling is the fun part. Sooner or later you get to the hard part – unpacking the bags and settling down to write. Getting started can be the hardest part when your mind is still buzzing with the sights you have seen, the people you have met. Sometimes it is better to wait for a while before committing your thoughts to paper.

You will have read many different travel articles during the course of your market research. Some you will like. Some will leave you less impressed. Obviously you will pitch each piece at a particular magazine, but although you must copy its style as regards format and length, you should still aim to be yourself. Readers are interested in your impressions and it is your personal experience which hopefully will make your article stand out from the competition.

Many of the general principles of article writing also apply to travel writing, but there are several techniques which will help to add sparkle to your holiday memories:

– Avoid clichés. Rugged mountains, shimmering water, glistening snow. They all conjure up an image, but they are tired and unimaginative. Think up some original descriptions of your own and really make the reader think.

Sights and sounds all help to conjure up atmosphere. They do not have to be pleasant, but they do have to be authentic. If the aroma of a Mediterranean city in high summer is one of sewers and sweat, then say so.

– People make places, so always try to include at least one or two elements of human interest. A line or two of dialogue may be all that are needed to convey the attitude of an entire population – a quote from a taxi driver, for instance, or a market trader. Or perhaps there is a figure from history who had some long-lasting effect on contemporary life. Look for the people angle in everything.

– Any tourist can look up information in a guidebook. So present your readers with something slightly more offbeat. Delve deeper at the library before you go and explore the unusual once you get there. Look for the sights that other tourists miss.

– Never try to include all your material in one article. Write several. Choose your own personal highlights – perhaps along a theme – for each one. Be specific and stick to it. Ramble and you lose credibility.

– Your readers will not necessarily like what you like, so show them rather than tell them and enable them to make up their own mind. Entertain them into the bargain and they will have made an informed decision based on an enjoyable and authoritative read.

– Do not clutter your copy with basic details. Information

163

about travel options, tour operators, vaccinations, costs and best buys can all be neatly parcelled in a sidebar or two. They make the article easier to read and the printed page more attractive.

– Make sure your pictures are clearly captioned. Note down location details as you shoot them. By the time you have the film processed, you may not remember the name of that quiet little cove away from the usual tourist beat. And nothing lets a good travel article down more than incorrect photographs. The editor may not spot the mistake, but there is bound to be at least one reader who knows the destination intimately...

– Let your feelings for a place show clearly through the copy. You do not have to like everything about a place or its people, but hopefully you will like it enough to recommend it to others, or at least certain aspects of it. Be honest but constructive and perhaps the editor will allow you to convince his readers too.

9
INTERVIEWING

PERSONALITIES SELL

We all like to read about other people. Their experiences, achievements and their private lives. Pick up almost any magazine and you will find at least one feature based on a personality interview. Women's magazines, in particular, often carry a selection.

Many are profiles of well known people – tv and moviestars, authors, sportsmen, and public figures – but alongside the famous names, you will find more and more 'human interest' stories. These include anything from a woman working in a man's world to a family's fight against illness; an uplifting tale of childhood courage to an inspiring account of a battle against bureaucracy.

Personality profiles and human interest stories are big business in the magazine world and if you can come up with the stories, you should have no shortage of editors willing to buy them. For interviews do not appear only in the women's press. They pop up in hobby titles and how-to magazines, trade publications and the business press. Whatever your area of interest, there are always strong personalities who would make rivetting reading.

If you have never done an interview before, you may find the prospect a bit daunting. But so long as you have done your homework properly and know the market you are writing for, there is no reason why you cannot ask the sort of questions that readers would ask themselves. All you have to do then – in theory at least – is to write it up.

Interviewing is a fascinating – and addictive – way to earn money. No other form of journalism gives a writer access to so many different people with so many interesting things to say. In fact most people have some sort of interesting story to tell, so the experienced interviewer need never run out of feature ideas. Many personalities can also be angled to a variety of markets, which all adds up to more sales.

Celebrity interviewing is not a way of life for the star-struck or the tongue-tied. You need to be at ease with people from all walks of life and be able to ask intelligent questions, often under difficult circumstances. And of course you must be able to project your interviewee in a way that is compelling to read on the printed page.

But the more people you talk to, the easier it becomes. Honestly. And anyway, nobody expects you to tackle a Hollywood legend on your first outing. Think through your friends and contacts. There may be somebody close to home – and easy to talk to – on whom you can practise your craft.

There are, of course, many writers who have no interest in selling interview pieces. Nevertheless, it is still well worth fine-tuning your interview skills. All article writers need to talk to people in the course of their research and it helps if you know how to get the best from them.

There are also very few subjects which cannot be brought to life with a dash of human interest. A few quotes from a museum curator will immediately brighten up an article on hidden treasures. A paragraph or two from a local farmer can add weight to your feature on river pollution. So treat each face-to-face encounter as an interview and make the most of every gem of information that comes your way.

Before you know it, you could find you have changed your how-to piece on collecting antiques into an interview with a celebrated collector. Or even written both. Two potential sales and a whole new approach to working.

FINDING A SUBJECT

Before you can write an interview piece, you obviously need to find someone worth interviewing. Fortunately this is not nearly as difficult as it sounds. If you are already established in certain market areas, it is worth training yourself to spot interview ideas to fit those markets; if you are just starting out on your writing career, interviews could be the way to get established.

A surprising number of ideas can come from within your own circle of contacts. Let us presume, for example, that your hobby is fishing. You belong to a local anglers club and sometimes take part in competitions.

Think of all the people you come into contact with – fellow anglers, competition judges, countryside wardens, and so on. Is one fisherman always up among the prizewinners? Has someone developed a revolutionary new technique? Can you ask a well known judge to give some competition tips?

Or perhaps you belong to a particular trade association. Can you ask a successful businessman for his commercial philosophy? Is there a woman holding high office in a male-dominated industry? Or could you interview someone about training and career progression within your particular line of work?

Another good source of interview subjects is the local paper. An unusual small business, perhaps. A unique nursery school. A housing scheme for the unemployed. There is a personality behind every one, so make it your job to find him and ask about his enterprise.

Or perhaps you have a national celebrity living in your town. If so, the local paper is the perfect way to find out about his interests and activities. If, for example, he is pictured opening a new nature reserve for the area conservation group, you may have a story which may not be widely known to a national audience. You may also find that he is happy to talk about something other than his latest book or film.

Just as local papers can provide interesting interview subjects, so too can the national press. A short item on, for example, a new educational policy might provide you with an interview idea for a full-length feature. Talk to the person who formulated the policy or someone directly affected by it. Or both for a really balanced story.

Television and radio are an excellent source of interview subjects, especially the magazine programmes and chat shows. They deal with topical people and issues, and provide all sorts of ideas for celebrity interviews, human interest stories, and people behind the news. And because they give the viewer all the essential information, they do a lot of your research work for you.

Unfortunately magazine lead times mean that some of the stories may be past their sell-by date by the time you can get the interview done and down on paper. It is no good approaching a television star for an interview about his latest series if the show will be off air by the time the piece makes print. You need to be topical if you are to sell the piece. So if you want advance warning of forthcoming television programmes, it is worth making a regular phone call to the TV company's press office.

Finally, make use of your professional contacts as a writer. Public relations companies you have already dealt with, press officers, and so on. Make sure they know you are looking for interview subjects. They will be anxious to gain publicity for their clients and should be able to provide you with some potential storylines.

FINDING A MARKET

Market before manuscript. That basic principle of article writing applies to interviews as well. In fact more so. Magazines approach interviews in very different ways, so you must be thoroughly familiar with their approach before you start.

The angle is all important. A magazine for the over-50s, for instance, may want a straightforward career profile with as much 'at home' information as you can get. A mass circulation women's magazine, on the other hand, may only be interested in an exclusive insight into a star's marriage/divorce/love life.

And of course the sort of celebrity who slots neatly into the magazine for older readers, may not be of interest to a younger audience. So make sure your chosen celebrity is right for your target publication.

Then there is the question of style. One magazine may publish a 1,500-word profile which makes good use of original quotes, interspersed with narrative. Another may go for a similar length but favour a reporting style, using no quotes at all.

Some magazines publish a series of interviews along a theme. My weekend. My family. My favourite hobby. But whilst some of these are written entirely in the first person – as though the subject himself is speaking throughout – others will involve both narrative and quotes.

Then again there are the filler interviews – perhaps half a page with a picture or a few short questions and answers. Hardly a challenge to the writer, but well paid for the work involved.

If you are aiming at a magazine which favours a longer profile, make sure you read several of them to get a feel for the amount of author intervention. Does the editor like the interviewer to drop in his own impressions or opinions? If so, is he happy for the personal pronoun 'I' to creep in, or does he prefer a factual observation such as:

'Face to face, she is even more attractive and approachable than she appears on television – relaxed, friendly and very much the grown-up girl next door.'

Market study is essential if you are to get the best possible interview for your target market. The most interesting personality in the world will not sell if you approach the magazine with the wrong style of interview. Or the wrong personality.

But it can also be important from the point of view of actually securing an interview. Whilst a local businessman or a hobby enthusiast may be happy to give up his time to you, a busy celebrity – much in demand from other magazines – can afford to pick and choose.

It is therefore in your own interests to try and arouse an editor's interest before you contact your subject. If he knows your work, he may be happy to give you a firm commission; if you are new contributor, he is unlikely to commit himself until he has seen your finished copy.

But if you can approach a personality and say that you wish to interview him for a particular title, you stand far more chance of being granted an interview than if you are simply a freelance with no particular prospect of a sale.

LOCATING YOUR SUBJECT

There are several ways of tracking down your subject, depending on what line of business they are in and how well-known they are. One of the following should produce results:

– The copy of *Who's Who* in your local library gives biographical details and contact addresses for a wealth of personalities from all walks of life.

– Your library should also stock – or have access to – one or more showbusiness directories, such as *Spotlight*. These list actors, actresses and their agents, and are particularly useful for film personalities who may be less easy to get hold of than television celebrities.

Unfortunately, agents are not always as helpful as they might be to journalists – after all their job is to get work for their client, not help you with yours – but ask politely and most of them will point you in the right direction, albeit grudgingly.

– Television and radio press offices will be able to help with stars of programmes currently on the air or in production. They may be able to fix up an interview on your behalf. If not, they can always direct you to the independent film company or public relations firm handling the production. Of course, you could also end up back at the agent...

– Publishers' press offices are always happy to arrange author interviews. Get yourself on their catalogue mailing list so you know what new titles are due for publication. If the author is a popular one, you may have to join the queue, but if you can find a market for a profile of someone outside the main publicity budget, you might end up with an exclusive interview.

– Local papers can help with stories they have covered. So if you have spotted a potential interviewee in the local press, phone the news desk and ask if they can tell you where to reach them. Alternatively, if enough detail is given in the story, try the telephone directory.

MAKING CONTACT

You have found your potential interviewee. Now all you have to do is persuade him to talk to you. Most 'ordinary' people – in other words, non-celebrities – are happy to help, especially if they have a cause, a campaign or a business to publicise.

Celebrities can be more difficult. Many of them have genuinely limited time to give to journalists; others avoid over-exposure by giving only a selected number of interviews. If so, you will need to come up with a pretty strong case if you are to be given an audience.

There are two ways you can make contact – directly or indirectly. Neither gives guaranteed success but there are times when one approach is more appropriate than the other.

• The direct approach
As a general rule, you will contact most potential subjects yourself, either by letter or telephone.

Letters give you time to think out the most persuasive argument and give your subject time to consider your request. But they may also take time to be answered. Phone calls are more immediate, but are not recommended for those of nervous disposition. Catch your subject at the wrong moment, present your request in the wrong way, and your request may be turned down.

Whether you are writing or telephoning, you should give your subject the following information:

• The name of the publication you are writing for. If you already have a commission – or even a go-ahead on spec – say so.

• The sort of readership it is aimed at, especially if it is a publication which he or she might not be familiar with. You might even enclose a sample copy.

171

- Why you want to do the interview.

- How long you will need.

- When you would like to do it, mentioning any magazine deadlines.

- Whether you will be taking photographs, taking a photographer, or are hoping to borrow from your subject.

- Whether copy will be checked prior to publication.

There are two schools of thought about checking copy. Some journalists argue that it goes against the freedom of the press which, of course, is true, but unless you are planning a sensational scoop for the Sunday tabloids, you have more to gain by offering to check copy with your interviewee.

A few magazine publishers have a policy of seeking copy approval from anyone who is interviewed. If yours is not one of them, you will gain a few Brownie points by offering to let your subject see it. Few people will alter your style or observations, only incorrect matters of fact. And some well known people, tired of being misquoted by less conscientious journalists, will only agree to an interview if they see copy anyway.

Any technical content should always be checked, especially if you are using the interview for research purposes. It is very easy to over-simplify or misinterpret something of a technical nature, so make sure your research works for you, not against.

If you are requesting an interview by letter, it is courteous to enclose an sae. If you are using the phone, remember the telephone techniques listed in Chapter 7 on approaching an editor. Have everything you want to say – or ask – written down in front of you, make yourself comfortable and relax. They can only say no.

Finally, remember that some people are wary or nervous about meeting the press. It is often better to avoid using the words 'interview' or 'journalist'. They are far more likely to agree to an 'informal chat'.

– Indirect approach

This kind of approach is generally reserved for celebrities and other well known public figures. Showbusiness personalities have agents; business entrepreneurs have secretaries; and all sorts of organisations have press offices. They are there to protect their client or employer from the public at large and that, for the moment, includes you. So make your request in the proper manner and you are far more likely to have a favourable reply.

The only other issue to be resolved early on is the question of money. No, not your fee for the article, but a fee for the interviewee. Some of the mass circulation women's titles do bid against each other for exclusive rights to a hot celebrity story or a human interest drama, but this rarely concerns the freelance.

If an interviewee asks for a fee, always check back with the magazine editor. He may prefer to let that one go. Most people are prepared to give interviews in return for free publicity so an editor will have to decide whether extra sales will justify paying a fee for the story. Either way, it is not your problem.

THE MYTHS ABOUT CELEBRITY INTERVIEWING

If you like the idea of meeting well known personalities, it is well worth getting yourself on the celebrity interviewing circuit. The magazine-buying public seem to have an insatiable appetite for celebrity chat, so there is a wide range of potential markets – not to mention celebrities to interview.

But if this is your first attempt, it is well worth bearing a few things in mind before you start:

– Showbiz gossip is the real icing on the interviewer's cake, the sort of thing that people want to hear at dinner parties. But celebrities can be disappointing.

An actor who is brilliant at speaking other people's lines does not necessarily have many original ones of his own, so do not imagine you are going to meet the world's most sparkling conversationalists. Many an 'ordinary' person has proved to be much more entertaining or admirable.

– Magazines do not set up celebrity interviews for you. Even if you are asked to do an interview by an editor who knows your work well, the actual approach will be up to you. He may give you a contact telephone number but you will have to plead your own case and make your own arrangements.

– Even if the celebrities themselves seem glamorous, interviewing them rarely is. Visit a film set, for example, or spend a day on a location shoot and you could spend hours just waiting around for the chance to fire questions between takes. And although the first half-hour may be fascinating to watch, it can be unbelievably boring watching the same few minutes shot over and over again.

– Interviews are not an easy way to make money. Celebrity interviews in particular. The more well known the personality, the more you will be expected to know about him, and this means lots of homework. If he is an actor, watch several of his films. An author? Read a number of his books. And if the meeting takes place at short notice, cancel everything else until you are sure you know your stuff.

– Celebrity interviewers do not spend all their time wining and dining. In fact it is very difficult to do justice to a cup of coffee, let alone a full blown meal, when you are trying to ask questions and take notes at the same time.

Having said all that, it is always fun to meet famous people in the flesh. But do remember that they are just that – people. They are no better or worse than the family with the handicapped child you wrote about last week or the factory worker you met this week, who has turned his garden into an animal rescue shelter.

Treat them with the same respect you would any other interviewee, but no more. They are talking to you because they want to. You are there to help each other.

DOING YOUR HOMEWORK

Never interview anyone that you do not know about or cannot find out about. Not only will you waste everybody's time, but you will not do anything for either your own reputation or that of your magazine.

If you are not a political animal, for instance, it would not be very sensible to try and interview a retiring cabinet minister. Leave it to someone who not only knows the background, but will also enjoy the experience.

However, it is not difficult to research most celebrities. If the interview was set up for you by a third party – a secretary, press officer or public relations firm, for instance – ask if they have any background detail on your subject. Point out that it will save you wasting his time on basic questions and you immediately create a good impression – as well as get the information you need.

If you have set up the interview yourself, you can ask whether there is anything you should read before you come. Unless, of course, you are interviewing an author when the answer will be obvious. There may have been an article about him in a specialist publication recently, he may have an award in the pipeline, or he may send you literature concerning his own particular line of work or interest.

Many of the sources which helped you track down your subject in the first place can also be of help – *Who's Who*, the local papers, friends, organisations, and so on. You may also have something gathering dust in your own cuttings library.

Of course some subjects are easier to research than others. Some are more enjoyable. Some are more time consuming. But however long it takes, you owe it to your subject – and your reputation as a writer – to find out as much as you possibly can before your meeting. The more information you can gather, the better the picture you can build up of the person you are about to meet.

You might also be able to ask some original questions. A celebrity, for example, who has just made a new television series may be faced by many journalists all wanting to ask the same questions. So if you want to talk about his favourite hobby, his pet project, or some little known aspect of his other life, you may get an interview which is different from the rest.

Think out your questions carefully. Start making notes as soon as you start your research. There will be time to prune them and polish them later. Think about your reason for interviewing this person. Is there a project you want to find out about? An achievement? An opinion? Ask yourself what your readers would want to know.

Make sure you have a strong closing question worked out. This serves two purposes. It saves the interview trailing lamely away and draws it positively to a close. It may also come in useful when you come to writing it all up. Sometimes your interviewee may come up with a comment or anecdote which would make a perfect close to your feature, but if not, you always have your closing question to fall back on.

Where would you like to be in ten years time? What is your most significant achievement? What advice would you give to your children? None of them startlingly original, but all of them guaranteed to do the job.

It is important to think about the way you phrase your questions. If, for example, you have to talk to someone who is not naturally forthcoming, you will have to find ways of getting round their shyness with the right questions. Basic rule is never to ask a question which can be answered with 'yes' or 'no'. Frame it in such a way that they have to open up. 'Tell me what it was like... ' 'How did you feel when... ?' 'How did you tackle... ?'

If the subject is an emotional or tragic one – as can happen with some human interest stories – you will have to be sympathetic but firm. Try and show that you understand your subject's emotions, but never forget that they have agreed to talk to you. They must therefore expect you to ask questions which may be difficult for them.

It is well worth keeping a few stock questions up your sleeve to ask if time permits. What is your idea of the perfect holiday? What famous person would you most like to meet? What is the most exciting experience you have ever had? How would you spend a million pound legacy? The sort of topics which might reveal another side of your subject's personality and could make your profile different from everyone else's.

THE NIGHT BEFORE

Careful preparation is the key to any successful interview. If you have done your homework and worked out your questions, you will feel far more confident and in control. So the night before your meeting, check that you have everything you need and that you know exactly how to get to the interview location.

Now is the time to look back over your rough questions, arrange them in logical order and write a few reminders on a prompt card. Something the size of an index card is ideal. Start with the main thrust of the interview, just in case time runs out, and save the less essential questions till later.

Never be embarrassed to take a prompt card with you. You may not need to refer to it, but the occasional glance will make sure you remember the most important points. When an interview goes off at an unexpected tangent, it can be all too easy to forget them.

At the end of the interview, it is perfectly in order to look openly at your prompt card to make sure you have everything you wanted. Far more professional than having to ring up later because you forgot some vital piece of information.

Make sure you have plenty of sharp pencils and blank pages in your pad, if you are to be taking notes. If you use a recording machine, make sure the batteries are charged and that you have sufficient tape.

Which method you use, depends on your own capabilities. Shorthand – so long as it is good – enables you to be selective about which parts of the interview you record. It is also easy to work from, as there is no lengthy tape to be transcribed before you can plan your article. A good shorthand writer can work directly from his notes.

The disadvantage is that you can be so intent on the mechanics of writing things down that you do not concentrate properly on what is being said. You also need to be careful not to lose eye contact for too long while you write. It is most off-putting for an interviewee to see nothing but the top of your head.

However, few freelances are likely to have shorthand and will therefore need to use a tape. A small recording machine can give excellent results, provided you position it strategically between the two of you and so long as you remember to keep an eye on the tape. A discreet alarm watch will make sure you do not forget to turn the cassette over.

A few interviewees – including some well known personalities – are uncomfortable with a recording machine, but most of them soon forget it is there. You are unlikely to be told not to use it, though I was once forbidden to use shorthand and presented with a small recorder instead.

The advantage of using a tape is that you record every word of the exchange. This is also the disadvantage. If the interview is particularly relaxed and slow moving, you could find yourself faced with a two-hour tape to transcribe at the end of it. But at least you know exactly what your subject said.

Even if you use a tape, it is still a good idea to take a pad to jot down the salient points. Then, should the machine fail for any reason, you do at least have something to jog the old grey cells. If you cannot do shorthand, devise some short-cuts of your own.

There are some journalists who rely entirely on their memory at interviews, but this is risky. You need an exceptionally retentive brain to remember every single thing that was said and it can be dangerous to paraphrase. Some people, for instance, have such an individual turn of phrase that to alter their words would not give a true portrayal.

While you are checking your equipment, do not forget your photographic gear. Make sure you have plenty of film and that your camera and flash batteries are fully charged. It is far better to take too much equipment than too little – you can always bring it home. If you own two cameras, take them both. Every photojournalist has a horror story to tell of the day the camera failed.

Take along a back copy of your target publication – preferably an issue with some of your work in. Celebrities, in particular, cannot be expected to know every magazine which may want to interview them and it is only good manners to show them what kind of magazine you are representing.

And remember that you are a representative. Spare a thought to what you wear. Dress according to the type of magazine you are writing for, the sort of person you are interviewing, and the circumstances under which you are doing the interview. If you are meeting a smart television presenter at an elegant hotel, do not turn up in your jeans. Save them for the day you talk to a wildlife photographer in the field or go off on location with an outside broadcast crew.

Make sure you know exactly where you are going and how long it will take to get there. Then be as punctual as possible. Arriving dead on the dot can be difficult, but never be so early that you embarrass your interviewee or so late that you keep them waiting.

Work your route out carefully and allow leeway for transport delays, parking the car, and any other variable factors. It is far better to arrive an hour early and spend the time in a local cafe than it is to be an hour late and find your subject has left for his next appointment. If you are unavoidably delayed, always phone ahead to warn of your late arrival.

Finally, never assume that you will just sit comfortably opposite your subject and ask questions. Interviewers need to think on their feet – sometimes literally.

If, for example, you are going to interview someone who runs an animal shelter, you will probably find yourself talking while you tour the facilities. Go to the home of a busy personality and you may have to ask questions between interruptions from telephone calls and visitors. Talk to an actor and you could find yourself perching in the corner of a cramped studio surrounded by noisy production staff.

It is up to you to ignore the distractions and make the best of the opportunity. The circumstances may not be ideal, but the experienced interviewer will always manage to turn them to his advantage.

There are, of course, times when you will come away disappointed. If, for example, you are invited to attended a press conference along with many other journalists, you may have the chance to ask only one or two questions of your own.

Do not be content with merely recording the same answers as all your fellow journalists. Be firm. If you have a definite commission in hand, ask the organisers for a one-to-one interview with your subject. Even ten minutes alone together will give you the chance to explore angles of specific interest to your readership. You can then back this up with the information common to everybody. If this cannot be done on the day, ask whether you can arrange a private interview for another time, either in person or over the phone.

ON THE DAY

You have arrived on time and your subject is almost ready to see you. Use those few moments to take stock of your surroundings, whether you are in a television studio, a private home, or your subject's office. There may be clues to his or her personality. There may be ideas you can incorporate into your questions. Wherever you are, there will always be details which you can use to build atmosphere into your feature.

Start the interview off as you mean to go on. Be friendly without being familiar. Be positive without being domineering. If you visit your subject's home, you may be able to ease in gently with small talk about the room, the garden, or his pet cat. But take your cue from your subject. If, after the initial exchange of pleasantries, he seems keen to get straight down to business, be professional. You are not there on a jolly.

One inexperienced journalist went to interview a well known actress at a famous London hotel over afternoon tea. The actress was accompanied by her agent and the trio sunk comfortably into the deep lounge chairs to begin the interview.

Just then, tea arrived. Unfortunately the journalist was well into her second scone before she sensed that her companions were beginning to fidget. Could they please get on with the interview, requested the agent a trifle frostily. Her client really did not have all day. Nor did she give the writer the scoop interview she had hoped for. So remember, you are there to do a job of work. Get on with it.

Before you ask the first question, there are two very important things to get out of the way. First of all, check how much time your subject has available. You may have asked his secretary for an hour, but he may have slotted in something else. Nothing is worse than being half-way through your questions and having your interviewee draw the meeting to an abrupt close.

Secondly, you should reiterate who you are writing for and, if you have not already sent a sample copy, show your subject the magazine in question. Say whether or not copy is to be checked with him and, if appropriate, what issue the article is scheduled for.

Then take a deep breath, relax and get going. It is usually best to start with the main focus of the interview – the latest project or campaign, for instance. Get those questions out of the way, before you diverge onto less crucial topics.

If your subject digresses, you may need to keep an eye on your prompt card to make sure none of your important questions are overlooked. But do not try and steer your subject back on course unless you are quite sure they are off on a topic of no interest to you. Some of the best quotes and anecdotes come when people are talking about subjects which interest them, rather than those which interest you. So let them talk. You may end up with a totally original angle.

Always listen carefully. It sounds obvious, but you would be surprised how many novice interviewers ask a question and do not listen to the answer. One very well known television personality tells of the woman who asked how long he had been married. She clearly had not done her homework properly, but he patiently answered her question and carried on to describe the subsequent arrival of his son and daughter. She wrote down the answer, consulted her prompt card and immediately asked her next question – did he have any children? Not the way to make a good impression.

As well as knowing how to listen, the professional interviewer knows how to hold back. Unless you have your subject's agreement to talk about a delicate or emotional subject, it is rarely wise to push your luck. If you feel you really must broach a particularly sensitive subject, phrase your question as sympathetically as possible:

'I know you don't like talking about your divorce, but...'

or:

'It was obviously a painful experience for you, but could you tell me... ?'

Even if your subject declines to talk about that particular topic, he will still appreciate the way you handled it. And he is far more likely to agree to see you again if you should want to interview him again one day.

Make sure that you understand everything that is said to you, especially if you are not familiar with the subject matter. If, for example, you are researching some technical information from an acknowledged expert, ask him to explain the topic in layman's terms. Otherwise you will not be able to convey the information to your readers.

Similarly, ask for proper names to be spelt out. Even common ones can have different spelling – Katherine and Catherine, Philips and Phillips. Check book titles, names of awards, and anything which is not immediately familiar to you. Your copy will lose credibility – both with your editor and your interviewee – if there are basic errors.

Often a subject will imply an opinion without actually coming out and saying it. What you want is a positive quote. In this instance, it is perfectly acceptable to put the words right into his mouth. 'So would you say that... ?' can often elicit the phrase you want.

Once you feel the interview drawing to a close, ask your final questions and be ready to leave promptly. If your subject invites you to stay for another cup of tea or offers to show you the garden, accept his hospitality. You may well pick up some atmospheric gems to add to your copy. But never outstay your welcome.

Before you leave, make sure that you have an address for checking copy. Also that you know where to get pictures, if you have not arranged to take your own. Then offer your thanks and head back to the typewriter – making sure you have not left your umbrella in the hall.

TELEPHONE INTERVIEWS

Not all interviews take place face to face. You may require a short piece of information from an authority at the other end of the country. Or you may have to meet a pressing deadline for an interview with a busy showbiz personality. Enter the telephone interview.

Some journalists love doing them. Others would rather do anything else. You cannot soak up the atmosphere in a telephone interview, nor can you see your subject's clothes or body language, but there are a lot of advantages.

Provided you have done your background research properly, you can sit by the phone with the largest prompt card in the world and nobody will know. You lose the advantage of eye contact, but gain the opportunity to read shamelessly from your crib sheet. You can even spread cuttings all over the desk if you like.

You do have to keep the conversation going, because you are unlikely to find a subject digressing as much on the phone as they might do in person. But so long as you have plenty of questions to hand, there is no reason why you should suffer any of those awkward silences often associated with telephone conversations.

The same telephone techniques apply as for calling an editor and setting up an interview, plus a few more:

– Always try and arrange a mutually convenient time for the interview rather than simply waiting for your subject to call you. You do not want the milkman ringing the doorbell in the middle, the kids arriving home from school, or the washing machine whirring into top spin.

– When your subject does call you, always offer to call back to save his phone bill. Note the length of your call and time of day, so you can work out the cost of the call to include in your expenses. Most magazines will be happy to reimburse you.

– If you are talking to a celebrity on a private number, reassure them that you will not give the number out to anyone else and then stick to it. If your target magazine needs to reach your interviewee by telephone, call him first and ask whether he minds you passing on the number.

The big advantage with telephone interviews is their immediacy. It is perfectly possible to do a half-hour interview first thing in the morning, write it up and have it in the post by lunchtime. If you have access to a fax – either at home or via your local secretarial bureau – you can even have it on the editor's desk by noon.

WRITING IT UP

As you travel home from your interview, your head will probably be buzzing with ideas. Half-remembered phrases. Possible openings. Dramatic closes. Some people like to write the interview up whilst it is still fresh in their mind. Others prefer to let their thoughts settle a bit first. Whichever method you favour, it never hurts to sort out your material straightaway.

If you have recorded the interview, put the kettle on, take a packet of your favourite biscuits and get down to the task of transcribing the tape. If you have taken shorthand or your own style of brief notes, go through your pad writing out in full any words you think you may not read later.

Efficient notetakers try to leave a line or two in between each paragraph of notes. Then, when they come to sifting through their material, they can give each paragraph a heading in longhand. For the synopsis, they simply arrange the paragraph headings in a logical order.

The synopsis is, as always, vitally important. If the interview followed the order of your questions, then it probably progresses logically. But there will always be some important anecdote, some interesting fact that arose as an aside and needs including somewhere. The synopsis will help you see where.

Strong openings are particularly important with personality profiles and, fortunately, not too difficult to find. Interesting people have interesting tales to tell, so look for an amusing anecdote, an emotional human interest story, or rousing quote to hook your readers from that very first paragraph.

People who read celebrity interviews read them because of the celebrities, not because of the writing. If you are a fan of a particular personality, you are going to read about him whatever. You may well have bought the magazine for that one article.

However it is equally true that a writer may also persuade a reader who is not particularly interested in a person to read about him anyway. How? With a good opening paragraph which will intrigue or impress the reader enough to make him read on.

After the opening paragraphs you should briefly explain who the personality is and any topicality peg. For example, a famous TV star who has just written his first book; a mother who has successfully run a road safety campaign; a telephone engineer who spends his weekends as a Roman centurion.

A personality profile should never read like a cv, so having explained who your subject is, drop other biographical details casually into the copy. You do not need to list everything he or she has ever done, simply the major achievements and most recent projects. And of course a look to the future is always positive.

Any details such as organisations to contact, programmes to watch, books to buy, can be neatly boxed together in a sidebar. Aim for plenty of human interest, with tight writing and lively copy, and you will not go far wrong.

If your target publication favours direct quotes interspersed with narrative material, make sure the quotes are interspersed. Avoid large blocks of either quotes or narrative – a few short paragraphs are quite sufficient.

And never be afraid to tidy up. We all ramble when we speak. We use half sentences and too many sub-clauses; we make grammatical errors and change direction halfway through a train of thought. Transpose that speech on to paper and you will often need to do a little judicious editing, without, of course, altering the sense of the quotation.

You will almost invariably find you have much more copy than you need, so be selective. Pick the strongest anecdotes and the most relevant quotes. You may even have enough mate-rial to write a second piece for another market.

If you are writing two articles from the one interview, you must ensure that some material is exclusive to each. If one piece is a general profile, the other centred on your person-ality's favourite hobby, you should have no problem deciding which material should go in which article. If the two pieces overlap, one solution is to write the first person quotes from one article in narrative voice for the other, and vice versa.

The present tense can help give the reader the feeling of being at the interview and is a good way of bringing out the atmosphere of surroundings or circumstances. Take this example about former Labour MP, Robert Kilroy-Silk:

'Robert Kilroy-Silk is in a hurry. Again. We've met three times and I've yet to catch him when he's time to spare.

Today we have an appointment at BBC Television Centre in West London, right after his weekday discus-sion programme, Kilroy. He's just led a heated debate about the rights and wrongs of boxing and I'm hoping he's going to relax for a while over coffee. But I'm out of luck.

There are meetings to go to, people to be seen. Robert's on the move again, so it's straight down to business. Are all his days this hectic, I wonder?'

This type of approach not only makes the reader feel instantly involved, it also presents a thumbnail sketch of the kind of busy person we are dealing with. The interview took place in an anonymous BBC hospitality suite which gave the writer little scope for atmospheric detail, but by describing the circumstances of the meeting, it also makes the most of an otherwise dull venue. The editor of a national woman's magazine certainly liked it and so – it is worth recording – did Mr Kilroy-Silk.

All you need then is a good strong ending – perhaps that closing question you prepared beforehand or an anecdote which came out in conversation. Leave it for a day or two, before carefully revising to make sure the speech sounds natural, and the progression is logical. Balance the use of 'he' or 'she' with the person's proper name and vary the standard 'he said', 'she replied' with 'he laughed', 'she admitted' and so on.

Finally, when you have consigned your manuscript to the post, spare a thought for the person who made it all possible. If someone has welcomed you to their home or made time for you in their busy schedule, a short thank-you note is only common courtesy. Nothing too gushing please, just thanking them for their time and interest. You may also wish to enclose a draft copy for approval, unless it is being sent by the magazine.

POSTSCRIPT

If the interview sells and makes it into print, make sure your interviewee receives a copy. Check whether the magazine will send one. If not, do so yourself. A tear sheet is sufficient if the publication is particularly bulky.

It is always worth hanging on to your notes, just in case there are any queries after publication. If you used all the material in the article, there is not much point keeping them after that, but if there is still material left over, file it away for possible future use. Tapes are probably worth keeping, if only as a personal reminder of some memorable moments.

If you have not already done so, see if you can sell a spin-off piece to another market. A celebrity's garden to a horticultural magazine, for instance, or a snippet about their two hundred eggcups for a composite feature on collectors. You may need a follow-up chat to get all the information you need, but if you made the right impression the first time, that should not present a problem.

Finally, before you jettison all the notes or record over the tape, make sure that you have all the relevant details on file. Addresses and telephone numbers of everyone who was instrumental in the interview. You never know when you might need them again.

APPENDIX

WORKS REFERRED TO IN THE TEXT

Writers' & Artists' Yearbook (published annually by A & C Black)

The Writer's Handbook (published annually by Macmillan/PEN)

Write Right! by Jan Venolia (David St John Thomas)

The Penguin Dictionary of Troublesome Words by Bill Bryson (Penguin)

Usage and Abusage by Eric Partridge (Hamish Hamilton)

The Complete Plain Words by Sir Ernest Gowers (HMSO)

Harrap's Book of British Dates by Rodney Castleden (Harrap)

Directory of British Associations (CBD Research Ltd; Tel 081-650 7745)

ASLIB Directory of Information Sources (Association for Information Management; Tel 071-253 4488)

Willings Press Guide (Reed Information Services; Tel 0342 326972)

Whitaker's Almanac (J. Whitaker & Sons)

Who's Who? (A & C Black)

Spotlight Directory (Spotlight)

Writers News (Writers News Ltd; Tel 0667 54441)

INDEX

Subjects which merit a whole chapter – Ideas, Market Study, Style etc – are not listed in the index. Sub-sections of chapters are indicated in the index by ff after the page number.

* * * * *

A
'Aah' factor 94
Acceptance 16, 83, 117, 125, 129, 132ff, 136
Action plan 18
Adjectives 107, 116
Adverbs 107, 116
Anecdotes 103, 105, 116, 143, 145, 146, 148, 149, 154, 162, 176, 181, 185, 186
Angle 33, 34, 37ff, 102, 120, 122, 131, 141, 161, 180 (see also Multiple angles)
Anniversaries 33, 128, 157, 158, 161
Author intervention 110ff, 169 (see also Objectivity, Opinion)
ASLIB Directory of Information Sources in the UK 69, 70

B
Beginning, see Opening

Books for writers 63
Brainstorming 21
British Newspaper Library 68
Bullet points 86, 152
Business magazines 33, 149, 159, 165

C
Captions 126, 164
Charity magazines 9
Checking copy 172
Clarity 54, 101ff
Clichés 107, 116, 145, 163
Close, see Ending
Club magazines 10, 45ff
Commission 124, 136
Complete Plain Words, The 64
Contacts 35, 134
Copyright 29, 76, 132
County magazines 30, 34, 48, 49, 56, 113, 134, 160
County Records Office 68
Cover Sheet 113, 126

Cuttings 22, 33, 34, 60ff, 85, 124, 146, 151

D
Deadlines 44, 72, 77, 101, 115, 172
Description 104
Dialogue (inc Speech) 104, 105, 142, 147, 163, 187
Directory of British Associations 69, 188
Discipline 11
Discussion feature 144

E
Ending (inc Close) 85, 86, 91ff, 97, 117, 148, 184, 186
Eye contact 177, 183

F
Fee, see Money

G
Grammar 101, 105ff

H
Harrap's Book of British Dates 64, 188
Headline, see Title
Hobby magazines 26, 48, 49, 50, 56, 92, 101, 103, 141, 142, 145, 149, 165

I
Ideas book 22ff, 114, 146
Illustrations, see Pictures
In-house magazines 25, 42ff, 115

Incentives 18, 81, 99
Infinitives 107
Information Bureau, The 77
International Federation of Library Associations, The 65
Invoice 135, 137

K
Kill fee 135, 136

L
Lead times 33, 168
Length (inc Word count) 52, 109ff, 116, 122, 141, 146
Libraries 30, 34, 58, 59, 63, 64ff, 76, 158, 160, 163, 170

M
Mailing lists 35
Market data 56
Momentum, see Pace
Money (inc Fee, Payment) 17, 48, 57, 129, 134ff, 136, 137, 140, 152, 159, 161, 173
Multiple angles 37, 142, 153, 158

N
Niche markets 47, 153
Non-payment 136ff

O
Objectivity 110ff (see also Author intervention,

Opinion)
On-spec 55, 124, 130, 171
Opening (also Beginning)
85, 91ff, 101, 102, 105,
116, 146, 153, 184, 185
Opinion 110, 142, 143,
169, 182

P
Pace (inc Momentum) 104,
106, 116, 147, 148
Payment, see Money
Penguin Dictionary of
Troublesome Words 64,
188
Personal experience 23ff
Photographs, see Pictures
Presentation 125ff
Pictures (inc Illustrations,
Photographs) 74ff, 86,
122, 123, 126, 127, 141,
152, 157, 164, 182
Picture agencies 75
Press conference 179
Press office 36, 71, 72, 75,
158, 161, 168, 170, 173,
175
Press function 74
Press release 72, 73
Privacy 77
Prompt card 177, 183
Public relations companies
35, 71, 72, 73, 74, 75,
168, 170, 175
Punctuation 108ff

Q
Query letter 121, 122ff,
126, 127, 132, 139, 156

Questions 176, 180, 181
Quotations 104 (inc
Quotes) 104, 143, 162,
163, 166, 168, 181, 182,
185, 186

R
Reader identification 141,
146
Readers' letters 32, 40, 49,
51, 99, 111, 145
Rejection 11, 12, 14, 16,
109, 114, 117, 129,
130ff
Relationship features 78,
142
Review copy 73
Revision 114ff

S
Seasonal articles 156, 158
Shape 102, 115
Sidebar 53, 111ff, 153,
154, 164, 185
Slush pile 40, 129
Small press 10
Sparkle 15, 103ff, 105,
109, 114, 117
Speech, see Dialogue
Spotlight 170
Statistics 104, 116
Structure 101
Synopsis 84ff, 91, 98, 101,
102, 115, 124, 132, 161,
184

T
Targets 18
Tax 41, 83, 137

Telephone technique 121, 172, 183

Tip sheets 54, 132

Titles (inc Headlines) 112ff, 125, 126, 149

Topicality 33, 34, 36, 43, 121, 123, 127ff, 158, 185

Tourist board 28, 34, 62, 72, 160

Trade magazines 10, 42, 43ff, 145, 159, 165

Typewriter 11, 15, 79, 110, 125, 137

U

Unsolicited manuscripts 9, 40, 44, 119, 120, 129

Usage and Abusage 64, 188

V

Vocabulary 54, 101, 105ff, 106

W

Word count, see Length

Word-processor 11, 79, 107, 110, 125, 129, 137, 138

Whitaker's Almanac 33, 69, 188

Who's Who 69, 170, 175, 188

Willings Press Guide 69, 188

Writers' & Artists' Yearbook 33, 42, 44, 45, 63, 71, 188

Writers circles 18, 19, 27, 45, 49, 83

Writer's Handbook, The 42, 45, 63, 188

Writers News 18, 19, 46, 49, 83, 120, 130, 133, 188

Write Right! 64, 188